Praise:

"Nora is a hugely talented young musician who is following her dreams and spreading joy and happiness along the way. I wish Stéphane was still with us so he could enjoy her music too."

-Martin Taylor, MBE, guitarist for Stéphane Grappelli

"One of my favorite quotes by Milton Berle is, 'if opportunity doesn't knock, build a door,' and Nora Germain embodies this whole-heartedly. A passionate and hard-working artist, Nora never takes no for an answer. There is a great deal we can learn from her about pursuing our dreams with integrity!"

-Dima Dimitrova, violinist and educator; member of New World Symphony

"From the first time I played with Nora I knew I was in the presence of someone special. Very few jazz violinists have managed to balance the technical demands of the instrument with the ability to generate that thing called swing, and to achieve both without compromising either. Nora has this and how!"

-John Altman, BAFTA winning composer and arranger; saxophonist for Jimi Hendrix, Amy Winehouse and Eric Clapton

"Nora is a person who from the moment we met I knew was special, whose energy is charmingly contagious and unstoppable, and who I know will go on to do great and beautiful things, changing the world for a better future, one note, laugh, and loving smile at a time."

   -Michelle Tseng, violinist; alumnus of The Juilliard School

"Every now and then you come across someone who is in tune. I find Nora to be in tune with life as well as our deep, rich history of music that we share and enjoy."

   -Roland Guerin, bassist for Allen Toussaint, Ellis Marsalis and Marcus Roberts

Go For It

Surviving the Challenges of Becoming an Artist

NORA GERMAIN

ISBN: 978-1-4834-5810-6 (sc)
ISBN: 978-1-4834-5809-0 (e)

Editor: Liz Cole
Assistant Editors: Sharon Clews, John Aldhouse

Rev. date: 10/20/2016

Contents

Introduction

This book is meant for everyone. I didn't want to write a book specifically about jazz or about being a musician in my twenties because the context of this book is bigger than that. It's about life and staying inspired to live it fully, and as I've seen so far in mine, inspiration can come from just about anywhere and anything.

I don't claim to know everything about life or making music and I haven't yet achieved many of the things I would like to. I also don't claim to be an expert on writing biographies or telling stories, and I'm definitely not a jazz historian. But, with my limited experience of 24 years, 21 of them spent in the pursuit of becoming the greatest violinist I could be, I knew one thing.

I wanted to write a book to help and inspire people. I wanted to send a message to young people to go out and achieve what they want to achieve. I wanted to remind people just how precious life, friendship, and creativity really are. I wanted to help young people remember why it's worth it to struggle for their dreams, and to struggle for them with integrity. I wanted to reignite people's optimism for the world and for the trajectory of their own lives. I wanted it to have as much truth in it as possible.

The resulting book, the one you are now reading, is a bit of a hybrid. I'll tell you about my life as it's happened so far and then depart from that to tell you about some topics in the world of music, education and elsewhere that I feel need attention. I hope that you enjoy it in all of its quirkiness and honesty.

I don't assume you need my advice. I'm just giving it away because if someone had told me some of this stuff when I was younger, I could have used it. I can still use it! Whether you're starting out in your career and need a little encouragement from a fellow young person or you're much older and could use a bit of inspiration or you're just interested in learning something about me, I hope that you'll enjoy reading my first book. I'm not an authority. I'm hangin in there, and if you want to, I want you to hang in there with me. I read somewhere, "I didn't come this far just to come this far." So in the spirit of the long haul, I keep putting one foot in front of the other. I hope you do too.

Out Here

One reason I wanted to write this book is because I have been told over the years by many people that I am a little bit rare. Maybe they said that because I am a young woman playing jazz or because I play jazz on a violin. Maybe it was because I had a certain type of confidence or drive, or maybe it was something else.

It's true that there are only a handful of people alive who are playing jazz on a violin, and that is certainly a shame. It makes direct competition less common, but overall competition with everyone else, violinists and other instrumentalists, a lot more daunting. All of the so-called "fringe" instruments are thrown together and then all of them are judged against all of the more common instruments anyway. And being female, well, I'll get to that later.

I wouldn't call playing jazz violin a lost art really, but the truth is that of the handful of people that play this style of music on the violin at all, even fewer of them have a similar aim to mine, which is to share it with millions of people around the world. Most people do it for fun, or have added jazz to the ever-expanding encyclopedia of styles that non-traditional or non-classical violinists play in order to keep getting hired for a wide array of gigs.

To me, playing this music means a lot more than just filling some niche or defining a misrepresented instrument or gender. I live and breathe this music and feel that I have a responsibility to master it as best as I can and to inspire others with it. It's constantly flowing through my head, even as I write this. I feel the swing of jazz when I am walking down the street or buying groceries. I feel it when I'm whistling or snapping my fingers or clapping my hands. The feeling of it even made me want to sing it. I guess I couldn't keep it in any longer. The truth always finds a way to come to the surface.

Once the spirit of jazz found its way into my soul I learned the truth very quickly and it is this: Jazz needs to be cherished, shared and celebrated, which is a job for those exceptional musicians who are talented and passionate enough to give the music their all. That doesn't mean that I only care to play jazz and never anything else. I love all music as long as it's good.

Anyway, if anything makes me rare, maybe it's that I've lived my life to its fullest potential from a younger age than most other people. I've taken a lot of risks. I've spent the majority of my life so far solving problems and enduring trying times, usually on my own. I've always held very high standards for myself, for my art and for the decisions I make because I believe that having high standards is the key to creating the future that I truly want and not just a future that is a product of misspent time and energy. I know I'm going to make mistakes I don't see coming, so I try to avoid making mistakes I *do* see coming.

Another reason I may be a little bit rare is that I have never been afraid to seek the top of the top in anything. In jazz, that means hanging out with the greatest musicians. Being around people of that caliber is invaluable for learning and growing. The company one keeps is so important! To find these great people sometimes I had to travel, and travel far.

I was never afraid to travel long distances alone as long as I had my violin with me. Sometimes traveling was expensive but I always felt it was more than worth the cost. Money is such a poison. Nobody should have to choose between following their passion and eating. In that respect we live in a very difficult world.

I've had very little parental or artistic guidance but I've managed to find my way by relying on myself. Philosophically, there are three things that make up a person. They are the head, the hands and the heart. I believe these three things can take you anywhere you want to go.

Acquiring Wisdom

One time a family friend told me, "Nora, you have enough drive to move this whole dang house down to the next block." Sometimes people ask me where I get this thing called drive. I don't think that motivation be turned on like a light. Rather, I think that qualities of this nature need to be practiced and built up like a muscle. Even strong muscles can fail every now and again. Nobody's born with enough good sense to know how to proceed in every situation and there are times when you just won't have it in you to put in more work.

Wisdom can help you in these situations of uncertainty and there are choices that one can make that will lead to gaining more wisdom; things that I have tried to make a habit of over the last nine or so years since I left home once and for all when I was 16.

Hanging around people much older than you (in jazz that's easy!), exercising empathy and compassion to all people and animals, researching and listening to others whom you admire and respect, reading quality books, staying well informed about current events, seeking optimism and inspiration wherever you can find it, and making friends from around the world are all ways of gathering wisdom slowly but surely.

It's also very important to observe the destructive nature of the ego. I have found that listening to your ego, or in other words, believing what you think, will not help you become the best at anything. In fact, it will make you feel like the scum of the Earth. You can't listen to it and you certainly can't believe it. The ego is conniving and sneaky. Our ego judges everything we do. It sometimes judges us for things we haven't even done yet! It makes us regret the past and crave happiness in the future, causing us to miss life, which happens always and only now. In other words, the ego will cause you to lay more faulty road (a life consumed with thinking rather than living), which will only make you look back and cringe. Then while you're cringing you'll look to the future to try to solve what made you cringe in the past, always perpetually missing the present moment. If we can conquer the ego there is no limit to the joy and bliss we can find in our lives.

Out With It!

One great thing about writing a book is that you're able to get a great many things off of your chest. I wouldn't say it's been hard for me to do that. I have never felt uncomfortable or nervous about speaking my mind, even if my opinion wasn't the most agreeable or popular one. I've never hesitated to question other people's ideas or thinking and I'll admit that it hasn't always helped me to make friends. In the world there are haters and there's nothing you can do about that except not hate them back. Every hater is a person who was hated just a little too much.

I believe that we should all tell one another the truth without being afraid of how it will be received. We shouldn't be afraid to say what we think, and we shouldn't feel responsible for protecting others or lying to them to make them feel better. We all owe the truth to one another. Being respectful and polite is important, but telling someone the truth, really being honest, should not depend upon whether or not you think that it will be received and judged in the way that you desire. Just be honest.

In politics, education, religion and other realms of human existence, it seems that the vast majority of people are afraid to express how they truly feel. All around the world we see the negative effects of this. I hope that more people will begin to come out and stand up for what they believe in. When the majority of us don't speak our minds it makes the world boring, but even worse, it makes it oppressive, intolerant, mediocre and violent. It just ends up fearing itself.

When you do speak your mind, it often means calling others to question their logic. Some people have told me that I have an unusual talent for being able to help other people see what (or who) is in their way. Most of the time, what's in people's way is usually fear and themselves. If there is any way I can help you see what, if anything, is stopping you from doing what you want to do, then writing this book will have been worth it. This book is truly the best of what I've used to get myself out of my own way, and I hope that while you read it, you'll find the strength to ask yourself the tough questions, the answers to which may liberate you beyond prisons you didn't even know you were in.

Creative Spark

Though all of the other reasons may be true, the biggest reason I wrote this book was simply because I felt a creative spark, the driving force of any artist. It's hard to know where this creative spark comes from. As many of my friends and colleagues know, I am not religious, so I wouldn't say that this spark comes from a "god" or any such force. What I do know is that usually, when I feel a creative spark, it's best to follow where it leads. If you let it flow through you freely and without judgment (judgment means deciding in every moment if what you've done is good or bad), it can yield a tremendous amount of high quality material. The human mind is incredible, capable of hugely productive surges of creativity in so many forms. Look at Michelangelo's *David* or Gershwin's "Rhapsody in Blue." These are two examples of humanity's staggering artistic output.

I often feel that I am able to tap into some of this creative energy when I am asked a deep or serious question. Sometimes people write to me and ask, "Nora, should I quit making music altogether?" or "How can I have a career in jazz? I want it so badly" or, "I want to audition for this, but I know that I can't make it. What's the point?" I have always felt responsible to use those moments to help people as best as I can. I try to think of something that has helped me in the past when I've had a similar challenge. I try to put myself in that person's shoes, and when I can help, I feel honored and grateful to do so.

Since I was about 15, friends and colleagues suggested to me that I write or at least become an inspirational speaker. I thought they were all crazy! I hadn't scratched the surface of my own life yet. I knew nothing about writing and, at that point, hadn't the slightest idea about *what* I would write about if I were to undertake what seemed like such a laborious and scholarly task.

A few years passed by and I kept thinking of more and more things that I would put in my hypothetical book until one day I just sat down and wrote it. Finally I am excited and humbled to share with you some challenges, stories, and memories from my life so far, along with the best of what I know about staying inspired.

You may be asking yourself why someone so young would want to write a book. It's a perfectly logical question. After all, there are other biographies available about musicians and artists, self-help books about the creative process and spiritual guides about achieving your highest potential, all written by people much older and more experienced than me. By the way, if you want to, you can think of this book as a combination of all three.

There is a possible answer about why I wrote this thing, however. In addition to the reasons I already mentioned, I eventually came to the conclusion that my generation – the millennials as we're called, or as the comedian Bill Maher beautifully described us, "Generation Ass" – needs profound inspiration now more than ever. We live in a time in which high quality role models, at least in the mainstream celebrity culture, are desperately needed. Unfortunately, the focus of many famous people today is to flaunt wealth, fame and sexuality instead of to inspire in people the qualities that truly matter in life, like having a strong work ethic, being optimistic, having courage and showing compassion. The Jimi Hendrix, Stevie Wonder, Jascha Heifetz and Aretha Franklin types are very hard to find these days. The spotlight is not attracted to greatness like it once was.

Of course, there are exceptions to the rule. There are many outstanding people in the public eye who are motivating others to live extraordinary lives with integrity and I commend their efforts. All of the young doctors, inventors, musicians, visual artists, conservationists, scientists, activists, filmmakers and everyone else are doing great work to inspire and uplift people. These people are our future leaders. There is no doubt about it.

If you're young, you'll probably find that most of your inspirations are much older than you. That's to be expected and there's nothing wrong with that. However, the more I created and performed the more I realized that I needed and wanted a role model that was my age, or at least part of my generation, someone who could motivate me but who was exactly where I was. I wanted somebody to hang out with, somebody to confide in who understood what I was going through and who could offer encouragement and a few laughs.

I looked around and realized that there aren't many young people aiming to inspire their peers, either because they feel too inexperienced to help anyone else or because they're too afraid to tell others what they're really going through. Of course I eventually found many talented and hard working friends to share ideas with, but I wanted to go a step beyond my personal friendships. We live in a culture that rewards achievement more than it encourages hard work, and I'd like to break that cycle starting with this book. A lot of young people seem paralyzed by their own work, overwhelmed with their dreams and daunted with the task of succeeding in the ever evolving artist workforce on planet Earth. It's as if we're supposed to be embarrassed until we're millionaires, but when we're embarrassed we don't work as hard or believe in ourselves as much, so we take the wind out of our own sails. We become shy when we should be absolutely wide open and proud. It's especially important when you're getting started to be proud of what you're doing because you can't afford to pay anyone to work for you, so it's really up to you to light your own fuse. Ah, but there's a catch – you'll find that people will call you arrogant. Those people were probably too afraid to light their own fuse.

I'll be the first to admit that there's a lot of pressure on young people these days. Many of us don't know how we'll make enough money to live while we create and if we do, we don't know how long that'll last. Artistically, my generation has huge shoes to fill, and that's true in almost any art form, whether it's dance, film, music, or something else. Technological advances and the Internet have made it possible for the quality of content to go way up but as a society the *quality of content* is not going up. Meanwhile the entire world is literally watching your every move. We have to be increasingly more famous, more entertaining, and more productive on smaller and smaller budgets. And, for some of us, there's added pressure not just to perform well in our fields but to revitalize them for a new generation. And that's just the tip of the iceberg.

I came to the conclusion that being 24 and writing a book that is designed to help other people my age is both unique and necessary. Some of what you'll read is very broad and some of it is extremely specific. Some of it reads like a journal or a stream of thoughts. Some of the things I mention may not be important to you, or they might not make much sense. I'm an artist so many things I say don't make much sense to anyone. You may disagree with my opinions or form your own way of looking at things. However you receive this book, my hope is that there is something in it that can help you along your journey.

I hope to inspire those of you who like me, who are just now planning out your life's work and are striving to find your *own* creative voice. Maybe you're looking around the world and wondering why after so many years of hard work you're still not where you want to be. Maybe you're in school and you're wondering what the heck some of your teachers are talking about. Some of you reading this may be struggling to hold together your relationships with your family because your excitement and ambition has caused a sort of strain. Maybe some of you don't know how you feel about your talent or your life because the majority of the general public is not, at this time, very receptive to your vision or ideas. Maybe you're working on creating your own vision or ideas right now. Maybe you feel that now is the time to question what you have been told about yourself or about your art. *Let me tell you! I have been there!*

Some of you might be old enough to be my grandparents, and to you I say "Congratulations!" It may sound strange, but I have said before that I can't wait to be old because of how wonderful it will be to continue building on and celebrating life such a long way into it. I'd really like to live to be 100 and still be playing the fiddle. That would be a real accomplishment. Once I read in a London train station, "Never dread getting older. It's a privilege denied to so many."

Regardless of your age and whatever breakthroughs you are on the verge of making, personal, creative or otherwise, I want to thank each and every one of you for reading my first book. I'm thrilled to be able to tell you a bit about my life and how I've gotten myself at least this far. My goal is to be as honest with you as possible, and to tell you as much about staying inspired as I can. Of course, I'll never be able to tell you everything as words can only go so far, but in this book I've tried to go as far as the words can take me. I hope that in reading it, you feel inspired to keep your dreams alive, motivated to keep working, strong enough to trust in your own spirit and vision, and that this beautiful and unique inner strength spreads to anyone and everyone that you meet throughout your journey.

:|| 1 ||:

A Bit of Family History

"Hardship often prepares an ordinary person for an extraordinary destiny."

– C.S. Lewis

I was born on August 21, 1991 in Madison, Wisconsin, USA. My mother and father were both freelance violinists and played for some time in The Madison Symphony, along with my father's mother, who was a cellist in several symphonies as well. They are all still living in Madison but are more or less retired from performing. My father was a natural on the violin. He started playing at age nine and by 14 he was the concertmaster of the Milwaukee Youth Symphony. My mother told me once that the violin was easy for her also. She comes from a long line of teachers, five generations to be exact. If you include me that makes six! My mother is petite like me, and many people have told me that she and I look very alike. I especially see it in the hands. My grandmother, my mother and I all have very similar hands, especially when you look at them palm down. They're a Mediterranean olive shade and they are very muscular, but also very feminine and small. I'd describe our hands as tough and elegant.

My mother and father met at a rehearsal for the Madison Symphony. At that time my mother was attending the University to get her Master's degree in Violin Performance and my father was on a break from school. Aside from playing in the symphony now and again, my parents used to make money playing in what they called the Germain String Trio, which was one of the first freelance classical string trios in Madison in the

1980's. It was my grandmother's idea. It was successful by any standard, but due to a combination of stress from becoming new parents, my father experiencing attacks of stage fright and the shrinking prospect of making enough money to comfortably raise a family with, they took up other jobs once they had my brother and me. From what I understand, it was a fairly bumpy transition.

After taking a course on acoustics, my father became a violin repairman and restorer, also known as a luthier. He became interested in the subject because while he was a student he didn't have a very nice violin and my grandfather didn't want to buy him a new one, so he was forced to learn how to improve the sound of his violin on his own. He learned by doing, which is something I've inherited. My mother tells me that he is a mechanical genius.

Later on, my mother got together with some violinist friends and co-founded the Suzuki Strings of Madison violin school. She had been teaching for well over 10 years at this point, but now had a proper institution of her own. It became very successful and is still up and running, and my father continues to repair violins out of the house.

My paternal grandmother kept up her freelancing as a cellist for many decades. My grandmother's father and mother were also both musicians; one was a tenor in the church and the other a piano teacher. My maternal grandmother's family, who all live in Spain, is full of artists as well; some were wrought iron workers, some were visual artists or musicians and some others were expert Cava makers (the Spaniard's champagne).

My father's first cousin Bradley Bennett sang "The Star Spangled Banner" at the second inauguration for President George W. Bush in 2005 with America's Singing Sergeants. It was a hard time for our country and I in no way endorse the event, but I'm still proud to have a relative that was able to share his talent on such a big stage.

I have one brother and his name is Carl Martí Germain. He was born five years before me in 1986, and he started his musical journey playing classical piano. After at least a decade of that he took up the guitar and fell in love instantly. He once sent me a guitar in the mail as a gift, a cream colored Stratocaster with a pearl pick guard. He put it together himself! I play it a bit now and again. Carl has always been one of my closest confidants and we have a very strong relationship. He is extremely intelligent, resourceful and clever. He has been on my side during some of the most difficult moments of my life.

I wouldn't be the musician or person I am without his guidance and unconditional love, and I look up to him for many reasons. I have always appreciated his ability to think critically and to simultaneously understand many contradicting points of view. His knowledge of philosophy and politics has inspired me over the years as well. He currently lives in Seattle, Washington and plays and teaches guitar. He writes his own music and performs with many of the best local musicians, and he can play all sorts of instruments. On several occasions he's toured with his longtime hero, lead guitarist for King Crimson Robert Fripp, along with many other guitarists from around the world who are involved in Guitar Craft. There have been many different groups and "guitar circles" that belong to the international Guitar Craft community, and the way they perform is always stunning. Four, eight, twelve or even forty guitarists all weave melodies in and out of one another, darting between this phrase and that. It's really something.

Carl is the definition of a classic heartthrob. Between his knowledge of vintage cars, his wardrobe of sleek yet worn-in denim and leather jackets and his ever-expanding collection of guitars, each one with its own character and carefully adjusted details, I can see why the women love him so much. On top of that, he's intelligent and has an old soul. Good *luck!*

I have never performed professionally with either one of my parents, and when I think about it, I realize how strange that is. I have always envied friends who have musician parents who still play together as a family, who collaborate professionally or just for fun. Even so, I'm grateful that they introduced me to the violin when I was a little baby. Growing up in a musical house is to thank for any natural talent I showed when I was younger. You could say that I was born into a household in which playing the violin was a lifestyle, and I think that because of that, it was easy for me to have a natural interest in it and a desire to play well.

We lived on a fairly big lot with a yard in the front and in the back of the house, and just beyond the back yard was a beautiful green grass park. Directly behind my house was my elementary school, and up the road was the middle school. There were 100-foot tall trees in our yard and we lived walking distance to many beautiful areas like Lake Monona where I would sometimes walk after school and have a root beer by the water. My mother would cook when she wasn't too exhausted from teaching her students, but a lot of the time we ate dinner out of a can or the freezer. We never went hungry and I am incredibly grateful for that. The house had enough space for all of us and our street was lined with beautiful green grass. Our lawn was usually overgrown but I liked that about our house. We didn't have many expensive things, but the house was full of antiques and hand-me-downs that all had their own unique stories. We had a nice wooden upright piano too. In the winter it snowed and in the summer it was very hot.

My father had a small ski boat as well as a canoe, and we went on many adventures in both of those. I learned to kayak later on and always enjoyed being in the water. I've been swimming in all five Great Lakes! We never went to Disneyland or to big resorts for vacations, but my parents did take us on camping trips dozens of times, and we also visited a few places in Europe, which was great fun.

I learned a lot on those camping trips too. Depending on where we were, and we camped all over the U.S. and Canada, sometimes there was no running water or we had to pitch a tent during a torrential downpour or there were bears walking around the campsite. Camping was always a learning experience and it helped us to build a lot of character since we often found ourselves in environments and situations that required a lot of team playing and hard ass work. The boat would get stuck on a sandbar. The motor would give out. Our food would go bad. Your last pair of dry clothes gets soaked. Someone breaks an ankle. You want to kill the person next to you and you have to be in the car another 14 hours.

Looking back on it I really appreciated these experiences. I'm glad I didn't grow up in a family that pressured me to seek external validation from other people. My parents were never superficial. They didn't care about what people thought about our family or how we dressed or if anyone was looking at us. They never asked me to think about what others thought about me. My family was too down to Earth for that, thank goodness.

That doesn't mean our family didn't have its troubles. Our house was full of dysfunction, really. It was a quirky little house with many colorful and odd things, and there was always something peculiar going on. For example, I remember one day that my father wanted to move the upright piano from the basement floor of our house to the upstairs floor. Directly above the stairs was our kitchen. He somehow put the piano fully upright onto a thin piece of particle board, placed it at a 45 degree angle on the wooden stairs like a sled, and attached about 50 pieces of rope to the piano and the thin sheet of wood. Then he fastened the ropes with wood clamps to strategic places in our kitchen like the counter tops, refrigerator, stove and other sturdy places. The whole kitchen was a web of ropes, all connected by one central boat crank, the type of crank you use to attach a boat to a trailer. I'm not quite sure how it happened, but slowly and surely he cranked the piano all the way up the stairs.

Every week or so there was something like this going on. I would come home from school and find my father working on something, usually a violin or bow, eyebrows furled, glasses on the edge of his nose. Sometimes he'd come up the stairs and his jeans would be covered in sawdust. I would look at him and he would just look at me for a moment and go back to his work. He never really asked me much, but I could tell he cared about me. One thing I didn't realize in those days was how much focus he had. He worked for hours and hours without taking a break. He had an incredible attention span.

Madison itself had a lot of its own character. It was full of colorful, eclectic homes, a picturesque downtown skyline with lakes on either side of it, and was brimming with lots of art and political activism. There have always been a lot of hippies and farmers, and I suspect there were even more in the late 1970's when my parents were in college.

Apart from what I experienced growing up, I only know about the darker parts of my parents' history from talking to my mother about it over the years. Every marriage has its challenges, and I've always appreciated my mother's honesty and willingness to explain certain situations to me as best as she could. Unfortunately, my mother and father later took to drinking to cope with their internal struggles, and there were many. As a result, I feel like I haven't gotten to know either of my parents very well. This may sound strange and a bit paradoxical, but believe me. I feel that way too.

It's possible that things for them could improve in the future, but after a decade of trying to help them, I don't feel that it's my responsibility anymore. You could say I've let it go in a way. A lot of people ask me what it was like to grow up with two violinist parents, thinking that it was some sort of string quartet party every night. In reality, things were very different. My mother and father weren't cheerleaders in my life. They were typically worried about money and they wanted financial stability to be my principle goal. They didn't seem to believe in accomplishing extraordinary things and they weren't people to give advice or encouragement. They were simple people, people who didn't see a need to have an unshakable belief in each other or in their children. Even though they didn't show it often I know that there were times when they were happy for me.

When I was in grade school I would often spend time with other families who did things that my family usually didn't like going to dinner together or having a family movie night or going to brunch after a morning at church. My friends' parents would ask me about school and about playing the violin, they'd tuck me in at night and sometimes they'd ask me to play something for them on the piano or the violin. They had friends over for dinner parties and card games. They remembered things about me and about my life. They cared about how we felt and what we were thinking about. They treated us with respect, and there were rules in the house. They offered to do things for us like take us for ice cream or help us with our homework. The moms did their hair and makeup and the dads complimented us before they went to work. It was a wonderland to me, a wonderland of structure, compassion and normalcy.

Years later I can now understand why my father had a hard time conceiving of me becoming successful as a performer. He could see me scraping by but he could never envision a slam-dunk. It wasn't because he didn't believe in hard work or because he didn't think I was good enough, but because he had a general lack of hope, enthusiasm and optimism. It was the way he was raised I suppose. He saw certain outcomes of his own life as failures, inevitable failures, and here I was, seeing the world as my oyster. My big dreams didn't fit into the way he or my mother saw the world from their quaint, Midwestern house. In their eyes I was probably something of a naïve and overly confident idealist. I wouldn't say they stunted my growth or progress. I would say that the charge that fueled my desire to achieve my goals fell totally and heavily on me, and my resilience is a product of that charge. That charge became my life force but it also caused my parents and me to grow apart fairly quickly. That's why I spend so much time with my friends and colleagues, especially around holidays. They remind me of the brilliant and wonderful things in life, and they remind me of who I truly am.

Luckily I've always been the kind of person to rely on my strengths rather than succumb to my weaknesses. I've always cared a great deal for my health, to have good friends around me and to improve my talents on a constant basis. I know it's not always easy for others to stay strong in these types of situations which is why I've chosen to write a little bit about it here. You *can* stay strong, but you have to choose it! Ignoring a situation or living with it even though it's unhealthy is not being strong. You have to choose to face it. You can't live life avoiding what you don't want. You have to fight for what you *do* want, and sometimes that fight is one without allies.

I know that my parents love my brother and me unconditionally. They just can't always show it. I don't take anything from our past personally. There is nothing that they could say or do to me that I would take personally, because I know that it has nothing to do with me. The way they treat me and the things that they say to me have nothing to do with who I am and how much they care for me, and so long as I know that, I cannot be hurt. I can only try to repair myself with love and by letting things go. With all of that water under the bridge, it's been difficult for me to have a close relationship with anyone in my family, whether closely or distantly related. The exception to that is of course my brother Carl. Without him I don't know what would have happened to me.

In later years I can remember so many times when I would play a concert and an older couple, my parents' age or older, would come up and tell me how proud my parents must be of me. People would tell me that they were impressed with my talent and with my love for jazz, and sometimes they'd tell me that they wished that their children could be more like me! They would say things like, "You're a credit to your mother and father. Your name is going to be in lights, that's for sure." They would tell me all sorts of beautiful things and I would thank them even when I wanted to just cry instead. It took me several years to be able to take compliments from older people and not wish that it was my mother and father who had said those things to me instead.

Now, with all of this in the past, I remember to be thankful for friends and mentors all over the world, both young and old, who have filled my life with love. I'm thankful for a never-ending stream of music and encouragement from all of those people, and I'm thankful for being a descendent of some extremely creative DNA. My parents put a tremendous amount of effort into supporting me as best they could and I know that they sacrificed a great deal for my brother and me. They provided for us, which is something I am deeply grateful for.

I'm grateful for my mother's cooking, her love of art and music, and her passion for teaching. I'm also grateful for my father's love of the water and of adventure, his expertise as a luthier and his belief in conservation. I'm grateful that I've heard them both laugh and that I've seen them both smile. My parents taught us a lot, mostly by us observing them rather than by them telling us anything directly. I'm grateful that they brought my brother and me up with a sense of wonder about science, about the natural world and with a strong belief in tolerance. They brought us up to think logically and to live with regard to future generations. They raised us in such a way that we cared more for experiences than material things. They taught us to save money wherever possible and to appreciate the little things in life like a good meal or a beautiful sunset. While I don't expect it, I look forward to the possibility of the two of them entering a new, healthier chapter in the future, either as a couple or not. Through it all, one of the most important lessons I learned was this; never destroy the things that money can't buy just because you're angry that you don't have enough money.

My paternal grandmother and grandfather divorced when my father was young. My grandmother was a fantastic cellist and worked tirelessly for many decades, but somehow, I don't think my grandfather quite saw being a musician as a legitimate or respectable profession. I can understand that. He didn't know any great musicians so he, like my father, saw true success in the profession as idealistic.

To be successful as a musician you really have to come up with your own way of making money, but it certainly can be done. Like so many great musicians, my grandmother struggled to make enough money even with her talent and years of dedication. She got so many scholarships to go to school that she actually turned one down because she thought it was unfair how much money they wanted to give her! After I heard this story I learned how important it is to never impede your own progress.

Her ex-husband, my grandfather, worked for the Department of Natural Resources in Wisconsin and taught my brother and I about all of the different plants and animals we encountered on our nature hikes in Wisconsin. He introduced me to the wonder of communing with nature, something I have always cherished. He has received numerous awards over the years for his conservation efforts and he was also a student of the famous conservationist and author Aldo Leopold.

Still another musician in my family is my mother's mother, my maternal grandmother (we call her "Avia") who was a choral director and piano teacher. She studied at the Barcelona Conservatory of Music and her father, my great grandfather, was a violinist, too! Avia grew up in Spain, and lived most of her life in Barcelona, Catalonia before moving to West Virginia after she married my grandfather, an intellectual American soldier who fought in World War II. He has since died, and I regretfully never got to know him since I was too little when he passed on. Everyone tells me that I would have loved him.

Avia is always in very high spirits, even when ill or otherwise burdened. I am named after her mother, my great grandmother Francesca who I never met. Francesca was beautiful, charming, fiery and resourceful. She raised her children during the horrific Spanish Civil War and without her brave and courageous efforts, the family could have starved or worse! She took the train when it was being bombed and had to go from house to house all day to find enough food to feed her family with. Avia was a small girl at the time but her mother, Francesca, made sure that they were all safe and fed even if it meant going on very dangerous and sometimes illegal missions by herself. I hope that I have some of those genes in me. It's not how you live your life when it's easy that counts; it's how you live it when it's tough!

I love learning about what life was like in Barcelona (during the good years, of course). My grandmother has told me dozens of stories, and she taught me to speak Catalan when I was little. I don't remember very much unless I visit Spain, but I did study Spanish throughout school and like to speak it when the opportunity arises. My brother's and my middle names are Catalan. Martí and Francesca are two very common names in Catalonia. Martí is usually a last name, (and we have some Martís in our family), and Francesca is usually a first name. You pronounce Martí "mar – tee" with an accent on the "tee" and Francesca, unlike the Italian pronunciation, is pronounced without the "ch" sound. You say it like fran – ses – kah.

With her thick Spanish accent, my grandmother used to say things like, "if you are intelligent, you can never be bored" or, "we are women with hair on the chest." Sometimes, even in her old age, her enthusiasm overwhelms everyone. She is from a different part of the world and a very different time than I, and although our opinions can oppose one another, I still find her elegance and passion for life inspiring.

Here is what my mother told me about growing up in her family:

"When I was in grade school in West Virginia, my dad would get free tickets for the family as long as he worked as an usher at the "Marshall Artists Series" which was a series of varied concert artists that would drop in on Huntington. Avia would get us all dressed up and take us to the Keith-Albee theatre, which still exists in downtown Huntington, although it's now a bit rundown. Trips to these concerts were as cool or better than any Disney World attraction. The building was very large and decorated in a Moorish Castle Theme. There were velvet drapes everywhere, marble counters in the bathroom, lavish tiles, and when you sat in the balcony there was a faux ceiling with fake stars embedded. The design made you feel like you were in the courtyard of a castle looking up at the sky. We got to see ballets, operas, symphonies and it was amazing…I was all of 8-11 years old."

The rest of the members of my family who aren't musicians have impressive talents of their own. My father's brother is a wind power engineer and has sailed in a sailboat by himself from San Francisco to Hawaii twice! His wife made me one of the most beautiful quilts I have ever seen, a truly a gorgeous work of art. They are intelligent and progressive people and they live in Oakland, California. My mother's sister is a history professor at Marshall University in West Virginia and she is an author as well. The family continues and continues and doesn't get any less impressive if you can believe that.

My paternal grandfather, after he was divorced from my grandmother, married a lovely woman called Colleen. Growing up in Madison I knew her as my grandma. Unfortunately, she has since passed away, but she was a wonderful lady. She always made these fruity desserts with raspberries fresh from her garden in their back yard, which I often had tours of by her or my grandfather. I remember that she used to play Ella Fitzgerald on the radio, and I think that could have been the first time I heard any authentic jazz music. My mother and father played Miles Davis in the house a little bit, but hearing Ella whenever we were at their house really stuck with me. I can almost remember what Ella sounded like before I knew who Ella was. When Colleen died I was in school in New York, so I flew back to Wisconsin to play at her funeral.

Through it all, it is a great gift of truly immeasurable beauty that I have two grandmothers, both the mother of my mother and the mother of my father, that played the music of Bach and Mozart. I will never forget that. They've both made me really strong, and although I'd never wish the experience I had growing up on anyone else, I can't go back and change it, so I might as well embrace the good that came from it. For example, I am always very calm in a crisis.

Some people tell me that "everything happens for a reason," which I think is utter nonsense. Children do not get Cancer for a reason. But what I do think is that a challenging situation always yields an opportunity for positive growth and character building. In other words, you can always learn something positive from a difficult situation in life. There may not be a reason, but there is hopefully a lesson. Throughout my (short) life I've tried to focus on that simple truth, and in that I've found both peace and strength. Good thing too, because it turns out I would need it for the future.

:| 2 |:

My History

"I can be changed by what happens to me. But I refuse to be reduced by It."

– Maya Angelou

I began playing the violin when I was about two and a half years old. I started on a cardboard violin before getting a real violin when I was about three or four. I got into a lot of trouble when I was a little kid. I cut the hair off of one of my first violin bows with a scissors. I also stuffed one of my first real wood violins with Easter grass, that plastic shredded grass that you use as the bedding for an Easter basket. Luckily with a luthier in the house, my father was able to take the top off of the violin and remove it all. I will admit he had some formidable patience. My father's profession came in handy later on, too, because he was able to loan me instruments and bows to play on after I left home.

One of my first memories is sitting on a kids' "potty," the kind your parents give you when you're learning to be "potty trained." I was sitting on one of those in my parents' house in the living room. There was a small violin in my arms, and a plate of macaroni and cheese next to me on the floor with a baby spoon in it. I was watching cartoons on the television but I think they were on mute, and I was supposed to be practicing. I just remember sitting there on my potty, watching the TV, thinking about whether I was going to play another note or eat some more macaroni.

I was very active when I was small. I loved to run around and make messes. I painted and yelled and I refused to wear clothes for many years.

I loved to be in the spotlight, but I didn't like when anybody pointed that out. I still don't. I pulled lots of pranks on my brother and his friends and I went on lots of adventures in my back yard and through the neighborhood. I liked to sing and dance all the time. There was always a song stuck in my head. I got lots of "boo boos" (or as my friends in Europe call them, "knocks the scrapes") that were usually my own fault, and I threw a lot of tantrums when I didn't get my way. I was a handful.

I also remember loving the violin. There were times when I hated it and wanted to quit, but that never lasted long. I wanted to be great at the violin, and I remember wanting to know what my other violin-playing friends were working on, so that they wouldn't get too far ahead of me in the violin repertoire we were all studying!

I learned to play violin in what became a very successful classical violin school that my mother co-founded in the early nineties called Suzuki Strings of Madison. It started small, but now teaches over one hundred students each year and has hundreds of alumni. Aside from my first year or so on the violin, my mother was never my private teacher in a formal setting. She did teach me in other ways that were more intuitive and subtle, though. I watched her leave for gigs when I was a baby, and I watched her teach a lot of lessons. I studied her technique as a violinist and when we had concerts, she often led the group.

I had private lessons throughout my childhood with various classical violin teachers and during that time, after school a couple days a week, I would go to Suzuki Strings of Madison for various group violin classes which usually took place in a church that they rented. We learned basic music theory and lots of easy classical repertoire, and we all played solo recitals and often performed group concerts. We learned concertos for the violin by Bach and Vivaldi and played minuets and little show pieces, folk songs, fiddle tunes, pieces from soundtracks like the Theme from *Schindler's List* and other music, too. Most of the classical pieces were edited or arranged to be easier for young violinists to play which some people look down on, but I don't see any harm in it. Some people criticize the Suzuki Method as a whole but I really enjoyed being a Suzuki student. At a young age we learned an enormous amount of music by ear and I think that was very good training for my later years in jazz.

My mother also started a tour group called "Sonora Strings" which was a smaller group of twenty or so intermediate to advanced violinists and we traveled together around the Midwest playing concerts for the holidays and on other occasions. This was my first real touring experience, and I was about thirteen then. I didn't realize that I was on tour at the time, but looking back on it, the shows were quite professional.

I always appreciated that my mother and her colleagues were really creative year-round with the format and the context of the performances. I wasn't educated in a dry, tense, strict musical environment – we were playing in full on costumes sometimes, like for Halloween or for Christmas or other occasions. It was always a blast and my mother liked to dress up, too. Sometimes there was a bit of comedy involved in the show, which really enhanced the experience for everyone. My mom was usually the creative juice behind it.

I played in tons of interesting places like The Milwaukee Art Museum, The Capitol Building in Madison, The Monona Terrace, The Civic Center in Madison, various opera houses, theaters and concert halls, some music schools in Chicago and elsewhere, many museums and even outdoor functions like farmers markets, parties and things like that. Suzuki Strings also had "play ins" every so often which were informal concerts that all the parents would come to where we would review our repertoire and play it as a group. There were many rows of us. The little ones were in the front and the older ones in the back.

During several summers I played at a Suzuki violin summer camp at Stevens Point in Wisconsin, which was also where my mother trained to become a Suzuki teacher many years before. She was a student of the renowned violin educator Margery Aber. I also remember being about 12 and busking downtown near the Capitol in Madison but was asked to move by a policeman. After seeing that happen, someone walked over and gave me a $10 bill. That was my first glimpse into the potential generosity of the public.

My father would take me along to his appointments at violin shops or for luthier house calls from time to time. I visited all of the major violin shops in Chicago as a little girl and remember visiting the great jazz bassist Richard Davis' house in Madison. Richard was one of my father's music professors in college and my father used to re-hair his bows.

I also attended some master classes that my mother and the other faculty at Suzuki Strings set up for the program, and those were really inspiring. Hilary Hahn came to do a master class at the Boys and Girls Club, and another time, Mark O'Connor came to do a master class and a performance in a gymnasium at a local school and we all played one of his fiddle tunes. I still remember that tune more than 10 years later! My parents also took me to see Regina Carter, Sarah Chang, Midori, Jennifer Koh, Nadja Salerno-Sonnenberg, and many other great violinists and performers of all sorts whenever they came through Madison.

When I was around ten years old, we went to see Nadja Salerno-Sonnenberg play the Tchaikovsky Violin Concerto, which is one of my very favorite pieces of classical music. I think that was the first time I ever cried hearing live music, and I remember the feeling so vividly. I was sitting there, barely able to see over the seat in front of me, sitting in a row of kids my age with my mother and some other adults nearby. When I looked up and over the seat and slightly to the left, I could see Nadja playing right in front of me. I remember the sound of the orchestra playing in between her solo violin phrases and just being in total awe of her mastery. I also remember feeling what a lot of musicians feel after a moment of deep inspiration – the urge to go practice immediately.

One of my violin teachers was playing in the orchestra behind her that day and she picked up one of Nadja's stray bow hairs left on stage after the show and got Nadja to autograph a program for me. We framed it all along with the ticket stub and it was one of my prized possessions as a kid.

I probably would have shown more promise as a classical violinist when I was a young teenager if I hadn't been so intimidated by the need for perfection in the music. I didn't know that a few years later I would find jazz music and feel totally liberated. Back then, I was a bit in the dark.

I had some fantastic elementary and middle school teachers and recall that some in particular were very encouraging to me regarding my early passion for playing the violin. They loved it whenever I'd bring my violin to the school talent show or as an extra surprise for a school choir concert. One teacher who I remember being especially supportive was Mr. Eeg. Every so often I'd bring my violin to school and play fiddle tunes or classical music or things like that. He always asked me how my violin was going when I came in for class. Sometimes during school functions a teacher would interview me in front of all the students for about three minutes. It was good training for my nerves. Some of the other kids made fun of me a bit, but I always enjoyed the experience.

I had another teacher, Mr. Landry, who played guitar and sang wonderful folk songs almost every day in his class. I'm sure he wasn't supposed to do this as often as he did, but he'd put the lyrics on the overhead projector and we'd sing along to these wonderful songs, some that I still remember today! There was a song I really enjoyed called "Four Strong Winds," and another one that I think was called "Long Way Home," which was a song about all of the ways that you could find your way back home if you got lost.

Although I had support and encouragement from these two teachers, I felt a bit lost and frustrated throughout the majority of my elementary and early teenage years. I took to other forms of expression to keep myself motivated. I wanted to be popular so I tried things that other girls were trying. I took gymnastics, enrolled in swim team, did a few years of ballet and jazz dance, tried some Spanish Flamenco dance, some classical singing lessons and even participated in a voice competition for young students. I did some drawing and painting for fun, a bit of flute, played some piano, and also enrolled in some musical theater. In 6th grade I was "Little Cosette" in the local high school's production of *Les Misérables* and sang the song, "Castle on a Cloud."

I think that year was also the year my aunt Joan died of brain cancer. I knew that it was really hard on the family, especially her mother and her siblings. She was only in her 50's when she passed away. After she was diagnosed, her health deteriorated very quickly. I like to think that she didn't feel much pain and just went into a gentle fog that never lifted. I remember seeing her in that phase – she was able to sit up straight and walk around but she wasn't herself as I remembered her. Towards the end of her life I hated to see her suffer and remember visiting her in bed. I can't remember very much about it but I remember her very well before she was sick. She was a wonderful woman and I loved spending time with her when I was a little girl. She would take us all over Madison and we'd eat at diners, take nature hikes, and visit the zoo. I enjoyed spending time at her house and observing her cats. I will always remember her that way, really bubbly and full of life. She was a great lady.

∽

After about 6th grade, I was also learning some new fiddle music from the Celtic tradition in particular, and that strengthened my ears and my technical skill as a violinist a lot. In particular I grew to love a wonderful Irish band from Dublin called Lúnasa. They're all wonderful, spirited people and in my opinion, their music is the most uplifting and joyous traditional Irish music in the world.

Both the original and the traditional tunes were often played at really fast tempos and you had to learn them off the album. I learned this stuff just by listening over and over, internalizing what I heard, trying to repeat it, then getting it up to speed so that I could play it along with the CD. At first it was a slow process, but with practice it got easier. I was just learning this music for fun. I never thought that 10 years later I'd find myself playing gigs with authentic Irish musicians in Los Angeles or that I'd go to Shetland and have a jam session with the local Shetland fiddlers! You really never know how your early passions in life will help you out later.

So here I was, 14 years old. I possessed all of these seemingly unrelated artistic skills and a passion for playing the violin. I had no direction and no idea about what kind of a future I wanted for myself. High school had begun and I felt equally bored and disgusted, and it was starting to show. There were bullies at my school who got jealous of me and that didn't help things. I had become a nuisance in my violin classes. The tension between my parents and me was at an all-time high. I was frustrated everywhere – at school, in violin class, at home, everywhere.

I was seeing a therapist at the time and she looked after my wellbeing and my emotional and psychological health. She was also very encouraging and supportive, which I appreciated. I was angry with my mother and father and she told me that I was right to think that they ought to clean up their act. I was also angry about my other relatives' lack of supporting me in that desire. My therapist suggested I move in with another relative but when nobody would take me, I knew that I really only had two options at that point. I'd have to find another place to live on my own as a minor or I'd have to be adopted. I was only 15 then, and I really didn't want to be a foster kid. Plus, I knew that the whole process could have a terrible effect on my musical education, so I started to brainstorm about alternatives.

∾

During my freshman year, I was grieving the loss of a friend who drowned during the previous summer's annual camping trip on an island in the Northeast of Wisconsin called Rock Island. It was a six-hour drive and two boat ride trip from Madison. We had been there before, so I was very excited to return. Some of the other families on the trip had been going for decades. The night of the accident there was a storm that hit and some of the boys who were on the trip with us had gotten swept off of a sandbar in Lake Michigan into the deeper water. They were all able to swim to shore except one. We looked for him all night but were forced to confront the reality that he was probably in the water. In the morning his body was found.

It was a very traumatic evening for everyone that was there including me. At our campsite nobody spoke at dinner. All you could hear was the gentle, constant whisper of the flame from the propane camp stove and the occasional wrinkling of a tarp. Everyone was silent. I can remember trying to fall asleep with the red and blue lights flashing on the side of our tent as the Coast Guard kept looking for him into the morning. My father told me he loved me that night and I think that was the first time he ever said it. The weeks that followed were incredibly painful, especially for his close friends and family. He died only months before he would have started college, and I was only a freshman in high school. The whole thing shook me up. That was the first time I had ever known someone young who had passed away. I attended the funeral and the visitation a week or so later, and it still affects me today that I saw someone so young lying in a casket, someone who I had walked up and down sandy beaches with in the middle of the night, who I had deep and meaningful conversation with. Suddenly he was gone forever.

The day after the accident, back on the island, I decided that I wanted to go home and grieve but my parents wouldn't take me. They wanted to enjoy the outdoors and continue camping. Another family that came with us on the trip offered to take me home and they dropped me off at a high school friend's house since my parents didn't allow me to stay home alone when I was 14. I was so confused about why my parents wouldn't want to come with me and why they'd leave me by myself to grieve such a devastating event. It was good to have a therapist. She had a greater knowledge of right and wrong that was desperately missing in my life.

By this time my brother had gone off to college, so I was alone in the house with my parents for months on end. I was bored and the local high school influences were distracting and depressing. I quickly found myself at parties where I didn't belong and couldn't always rely on my parents to answer the phone or pick me up if I needed help getting out of somewhere. I was around boys who were doing things they shouldn't have been doing. I started to question my self worth. I was in need of some sort of purpose, something to re-excite me and to make me feel like life was worthwhile. I wanted a chance to become extraordinary, perhaps because I now realized how easily young life could be taken away, and I didn't want to waste mine.

:| 3 |:
What If I Go?

"The thing that makes you exceptional, if you are at all, is inevitably that which must also make you lonely."
                                              – *Lorraine Hansberry*

Without telling anyone, I researched boarding schools on the Internet where I could live year round as a minor and study music on a serious level. I didn't have anywhere else to go and I'll admit that I was scared. It was an uncertain time to say the least, but I was committed to finding a solution. The schools I found intimidated me somewhat as well, because I knew that I didn't have the background or the discipline that some of my classical violinist peers did. Some of these kids were practicing eight hours a day and going out for competition after competition. I didn't have a life like that. Naturally, I felt a little behind, but I tried my best to set my fears aside and I focused on creating a new plan. I found that there were three and only three boarding arts high schools in the United States and I chose to apply to Idyllwild Arts Academy at the end of my sophomore year of high school with the goal of attending for my junior and senior years. Idyllwild was in the mountains of sunny Southern California and the pictures looked beautiful. I loved what they had written about arts education on their website. They talked about how young artists have potential that needs to be nourished and guided, and that made a lot of sense to me. I was also impressed by the list of notable alumni who had gone on to do significant and fantastic things, just like what I wanted for myself.

By now I had turned 15 and I was well into my second year of high school. I was in the middle of applying for a place at the academy and I knew I would need financial aid so I wanted them to really like me. The application involved creating an audition video highlighting my artistic vision for myself that showcased my skills. I also had to write various essays about my life as an artist and where I saw myself in the future. There were several interviews over the phone and I mailed letters of recommendation from my teachers at my local high school.

In my video portfolio I sang and danced and played the violin. I was a bit of a mixed bag as a teenage girl but at least they could see what I so desperately wanted them to know about me; I had potential and I wanted to go to school there. I applied for a major that I didn't graduate with called "Interdisciplinary Arts" which was a program designed for artists who wanted to mix more than one discipline together. I was overjoyed when they accepted me. To be honest, I don't actually remember the specific moment of being accepted, but I remember in the weeks that followed how excited I was to tell all of my friends that I'd be moving to California. I was also given a large scholarship, about half of the tuition. I was very thankful to receive it, but my parents didn't think it was enough. After many weeks of begging, they finally allowed me to go for my first visit, which was the spring before I moved.

My mother and I flew to Los Angeles and drove in a rental car two hours from there to Idyllwild. When I got there, I was overwhelmed by how beautiful it was. Idyllwild is in the San Bernardino National Forest near Palm Springs, a mile above sea level. The sun was shining, the air was crisp and light, the sky was a rich, vivid blue, and the trees and flowers were mighty and gorgeous. From the moment I walked into the log cabin admissions office, I felt like I was in heaven.

I stayed a few days exploring the town of Idyllwild and I and got to sit in on some classes. It was absolutely fantastic. I hadn't even thought of studying jazz, but I knew that I would finish high school in virtual paradise, and that was enough for me to be excited. Also, during my visit to Idyllwild, I got news that my aunt Kathi back in Madison had just given birth to her son Gabriel. That was an added joy to the trip.

It was spring of 2007. I had just come back from my visit to Idyllwild and was finishing off my last few weeks at the local high school. During my trip I had been thinking a lot about an ex-boyfriend who used to live in Madison. He went to high school with me and while we dated, he lived reluctantly with his father. After we broke up, he decided to move away so that he could live with his mother in Los Angeles and we had been in touch every so often in person when he came to visit Madison and over the phone since he had gone to California about a year before. Now, with my move to Idyllwild only months away, I decided to call him and see how he was doing, since come fall, we'd only be two hours away from one another. I regretted breaking up with him and wanted to make things right. We had planned on rekindling our relationship -- at least that's what he told me he wanted to do the last time I saw him. I wanted that too. This time he didn't answer when I called, so I left a message asking him how he was doing and telling him that I missed him.

Less than 48 hours later, the phone rang and it was a friend of ours' who called to tell me that he had just died. At first I was in disbelief. I didn't believe him until he told me a second time. I immediately started crying and hung up the phone without letting him finish. I was totally devastated. I was so angry and upset that for days I didn't know what to do with myself. It was a shock to everyone at the high school and it was completely unexpected. My understanding is that he had gotten out of control at a party and had made a fatal mistake with a combination of drugs, medications and alcohol. I never believed that he did it on purpose, but the story had been told through the grapevine so what did I know.

It was a tragedy for all of his friends and family, some whom I knew better than others. It stayed with me for my two years at Idyllwild and I often think about him now. He was an extremely talented artist and he had a heart of pure gold. He was always smiling, always making everyone laugh. He often convinced his friends including me to go on wild adventures with him, promising a good story to tell later on in life. He was well informed, a deep thinker, a generous and optimistic person, a risk taker, and he was wise beyond his years. He was one of my favorite people. He was incredibly sweet and affectionate, and would go out of his way to show people how much he cared for them. Even as a teenager he wasn't afraid of grand gestures and he wasn't afraid of people knowing he did them. I miss him dearly.

Less than two weeks after he passed away, I reluctantly traveled to

Spain on a 10-day trip. My brother came with his girlfriend and some other members of our extended family met us there too. My parents stayed at home. I didn't want to go, but despite having to face this grief more or less on my own, my parents still wouldn't allow me to cancel the trip and waste the plane fare money. I was confused once again, just as I had been after my parents sent me home alone after my other friend's fatal accident on that camping trip two years before.

Normally I would have loved to visit Spain. After all I am one quarter Spanish, could pick up Catalan and Spanish fairly easily, and I loved the food, the dancing, the beach, the art and the architecture. We met my extended family in Barcelona, which should have been some comfort to me. Either due to the fact that they didn't know the situation very well or the language barrier was too great, or that I was probably awful company, this trip was different. I was alone in a foreign country with nobody to look after me, coping with the worst loss of my life. It was very difficult for me, especially at all of 15 years old. I remember locking myself in the bathroom, sitting on the floor and crying while I stared at the wall. Finally after days of this I gathered the courage to start remembering things about our friendship and relationship that gave me peace. I think that's about all you can do when someone passes on. Recall the past and be in the present with a light heart, face to the sun.

Months after all of this, a girlfriend told me that back when we were in school together and dating, he had planned to take me to see a concert at the newly built Overture Center which was the best concert hall in Madison. That would have been fantastic. He never asked me to go and I'm not sure when he was planning to, but she told me that he wanted to take me to something that I would like, something sophisticated and enriching. I was so in awe to know this. In this day and age, men don't really take women out dancing or to an opera or to anything like that. Some men can barely dress themselves for a proper dinner. But I imagined how wonderful it would have been to see a concert with him there. It would have been a beautiful evening.

He was a romantic, a true romantic. It's so hard to find one of those these days! I remember a time during school when I was sitting in English class. He came to the door of the classroom and even though everyone could see, he taped a sign on the glass that said, "Hey, Beautiful" and it was even typed! He went through the trouble of actually printing this thing in the computer lab. There was another time that he and I took a nighttime walk in the farm country just outside Madison and I waited while he climbed an entire water tower so that he could ask me to prom from the top. I was scared of romance so I think I said no. He was a heartthrob, a real California dreamboat. All of the girls wanted him but I didn't believe that he really wanted me.

I hate that death is so final. It's never too late until death makes it too late. Until death is involved, you always have time.

:‖ 4 ‖:

Idyllwild

"You can't use up creativity. The more you use, the more you have."

– Maya Angelou

F inally in late August 2007 the time came to move to Idyllwild. I should take this moment to thank Tara who was my admissions counselor. Without her guidance, patience and belief in me, this vital step in my life wouldn't have been taken. So thank you, Tara. You make it all possible for all of us to pursue our dreams.

I was excited and eager to move away from Wisconsin. Here I was, finally able to start my new life. In fact, I even think of my life so far in two parts. Part 1 is before Idyllwild and Part 2 is everything from that moment forward.

When I arrived, I moved into a dormitory, a huge two-story building with wide panels of dark wood on the outside. It quickly became synonymous with "home." It was called Husch (which rhymes with push) and it was one of the larger girls' dormitories with two floors and a basement. Husch was surrounded with tall trees and other buildings like it, and there was a huge field behind it where we hung out and where some people played Frisbee or soccer on the weekends.

I was really excited to get to know everyone in my building and in the other ones nearby. I got used to eating in the cafeteria and walking through the beautiful campus to and from all of my classes. I enjoyed my dance classes the most because they would finish around sunset and that was a great time to be outside. We all walked from dance class down to dinner in a big group, with our tights and leotards still on. We didn't bother changing and nobody judged us. That was the beauty of Idyllwild.

Almost every day I was going to a different event or concert on campus. There were art exhibitions, orchestra concerts, plays, recitals, dance concerts, film screenings and all sorts of things going on. Everything was going really well. I was exploring the school, the nature around me, the faculty who (almost) always wanted to help us when we needed something, and I started getting a group of friends together that came from different parts of the world and all had different artistic majors. It was great! We would all lie in the grass and get a bunch of makeshift instruments together and have drum circles. Everyone would dance, I had my violin, and we were free as the birds.

By the time I was a few weeks into my junior year, two significant things happened to me and they both seriously changed my life. I don't mean to say that they changed my life in the way that a pair of fantastic shoes changes your life or in the way that an excellent dessert changes your life. I mean these two events changed the *entire course* of my life! And, they both happened totally by chance.

I have always found it so interesting that when something extremely significant in your life happens, sometimes it's hidden in a moment that's as plain as day. Think of the way our solar system formed. A slight nudge in one direction or the other could have been the difference between the Earth forming or not forming. It's incredible.

In this particular moment on this particular day, I found myself in between classes or perhaps on a weekend stroll. I passed by a building near my dormitory and the music practice rooms. Later I'd come to know this building as the Hawkins Building, named after Marshall Hawkins, but for now, it was a plain brown building with many instruments inside. From what I could see there was a drum kit and a grand piano.

I met a few students outside who said that they were music majors, and so I asked, "What kind?" They said, "Jazz." I immediately wondered what that must sound like, what they practiced and what they worked on, but most of all, I thought that it was just about the most fascinating thing I had ever heard. So, after talking with them for a while about this jazz music thing they were doing, I wondered why I hadn't heard about it before or why nobody had mentioned this to me as a possible major. I suppose studying jazz violin is a little bit rare, and I admit, I would later become the first person to graduate with a major in jazz violin at Idyllwild Arts Academy, so in retrospect I understand why I hadn't heard about it. Violins belonged in the orchestra and that was that.

After talking with these students in the jazz program, I some way or another found a time to meet with Marshall Hawkins who was the founder of the jazz department, and also the founder of the Jazz in the Pines festival which took place in Idyllwild on the campus each summer. By the time I was a student at Idyllwild, the jazz program and the jazz festival had both been going for decades, so I understood right off the bat that he knew the school better than just about anyone else.

Finally I set up a proper meeting with Marshall Hawkins, and of course, when I walked into his door I had no idea who I was dealing with. This is the bassist for Shirley Horn, Miles Davis, Donny Hathaway, and one of the greatest living jazz musicians in the world. Not to mention, he became one of my best friends, a father figure to me, and would completely change my life. But in that moment, he was just the chair of the jazz department.

So I walked in and we talked for a few minutes. He asked me some very straightforward questions, like, "Why did you come here?" and, "Why do you want to be in this program?" I realized that I'd have to change majors and that was not a very easy thing to do at Idyllwild. Also, Marshall wanted to know why I felt so compelled to play jazz music, a question I'll admit I am still forming an answer to today. Finally he sat down at the wooden grand piano in the center of the room. He opened a fake book, which is a big book of standard jazz repertoire (you know, love songs, swing songs, bossa novas and so on) and put it on the piano.

We picked some different ballads (songs that are played at a slow tempo, like "Georgia on My Mind" or "Body and Soul") for me to sight read while he accompanied me with his beautiful and patient chord changes. My favorite ballad that we played that day was "Skylark," which is one of my favorite tunes of all of the many hundreds of standards I've learned over the years. And by the way, hundreds is only a *start* in jazz. Some musicians know *thousands* of songs, just in jazz alone!

Marshall also asked me to play some improvised cadenzas before and after the ballads. Those are little musical ideas, usually played out of tempo or "rubato," that give the tune context or setting. I tried soloing for the first time over the chords he was playing. This is actually the way I learned how to play solos. I always go slow, think of the melody, and embellish it a little at a time. I never think about the theory or the scales I'm supposed to use or anything like that, unless the chords are very complex and dissonant. Otherwise, I just play off of the melody. You could say it's a "Theme and Variations" approach.

Now, I almost always choose a ballad if I can only choose one song to play. Perhaps later in my life I'll come up with a new method for improvising, but I suspect not. Ballads are beautiful! They give you plenty of time to push and pull the phrases, to express your embellishments of the melody and to really listen to one chord changing to the next.

What he basically told me after that was, "You're in. Now get out."

Well this was just great! I felt so excited to start learning the jazz repertoire, to play in the 2pm daily rehearsals with the jazz ensemble, and to play in the concerts, which always packed the house. I was listening to jazz music and reading books about it around the clock. Stéphane Grappelli, Miles Davis, Ella Fitzgerald, Charlie Parker, Oscar Peterson, Django Reinhardt, Billie Holiday, Louis Armstrong, all sorts of stuff! Day and night! I was especially hooked after I heard Stéphane. I'm not sure when exactly I heard one of his recordings for the first time, but I remember the feeling and it was like biting into a juicy peach at the perfect temperature. It was absolutely magnificent. His sound hit me right in the heart and I wanted to play just like him.

Marshall would have deep, philosophical music lessons with all of us. He lectured us about life, energy, history, culture, about subjective topics like tone and feeling, about numbers like naming all of the things in life that involve "3" or telling stories about jazz musicians who we hadn't heard of but would go to our dorms and research after class.

Marshall is a great thinker and philosopher. He's a true intellectual who values creativity, discovery, science, compassion, truth, health, love, art and peace. The world needs more people like this. Young people are a little afraid, I think, to be profound in this way. Being funny and absurd is a little more popular. Nobody wants to get deep. Nobody wants to have a serious conversation. Nobody wants to think critically yet optimistically. I think the world needs more musicians and artists who are able to inspire with their depth of thinking.

Marshall talked about Duke Ellington, Ahmad Jamal, and Bud Powell a lot. He also couldn't stand the word "what" as a response to a question. He still can't. If he asked you a question and you said, "What?" he would throw something at you or start cussing. One time I said something and immediately after I said it I knew he'd be really pissed. I made a run for the door and he threw a fake book that hit me square in the ass just before the door slammed behind me.

Well, I knew even though I was taking his classes several times a week and performing as a soloist in his jazz concerts that I would have to change my major officially to jazz, but this was not going to be very easy to do. Luckily, Marshall was always very welcoming to anyone who wanted to play in the jazz concerts. I wasn't the only non-jazz major appearing on stage with the jazz majors. In fact, I remember one year a friend of ours who was studying a totally different art form was invited to play in one of the jazz concerts. He played a solo on the upright bass with just one or two notes that lasted several minutes. He got a standing ovation because it was so beautiful!

The second thing that happened to me in the fall of 2007 that changed the course of my life is that I met my best friend, Dima Valerieva Dimitrova. She had come all the way from Bulgaria as a young teenager to study classical violin at Idyllwild.

Dima lived down the hall from me in Husch Dormitory, and I had seen her around campus and knew that she was a classical violinist. I watched her perform a week or so before I met her with the Idyllwild Orchestra in Bowman Theater on campus. Everyone seemed to be talking about it before *and* after. She was a senior, a year ahead of me at Idyllwild, and she was one of the best artists at the whole school. She was a minor celebrity on campus and all of the boys had a crush on her. The year she graduated she won "Artist of the Year," an award given to the most accomplished and promising senior at the academy.

This all happened before I met Marshall, so you'll have to rewind the story a bit. One day I saw her walking through the hallways of Husch, looking fabulous like she always does. When I saw her in the hallway I asked her if she wanted to have lunch. It was the weekend and she had her violin with her as usual, and she was wearing a white summery dress and some white pumps. She was very mature for her age. I had short hair and a pierced nose and was coming out of a punk rock phase. She was on *another level.*

She told me that she was about to go and practice, but was going to go to town to pick up some chocolate truffles for lunch. So, we hopped in a van and went to the town of Idyllwild, a few minutes away from campus. We walked into the grocery store and she took about 10 minutes picking out the right chocolate truffles for lunch. We ate them together and talked for a bit. I told her that I needed a violin teacher and that I probably wasn't good enough to take lessons with the regular violin teacher that all of the classical violinists took lessons with. I also told her that if she didn't teach me I was probably going to quit violin altogether. I told her that she was my last hope.

She agreed to teach me a little bit, so we met every week or so for some lessons and she helped to sharpen my skills and lift my spirit. Before a month passed we were inseparable. She was learning English at the time and I remember once she wrote "no slirts" in my music instead of "no slurs." We'd meet in each other's rooms and talk all night, share our musical tastes and talk about what life was like at home before coming to Idyllwild. We talked about the boys we liked and the boys that liked us, how classes were going and so on and so forth. We laughed together, cried together, practiced together -- it was a hell of a time.

We always left little uplifting notes for one another, ate together in the cafeteria when our schedules were similar, spent the weekends in the sun, ran through the snow in the winter, visited our favorite restaurants and shops and talked about going to college. The whole year flew by! In our lessons we worked on all sorts of wonderful music. She gave me Bulgarian folk songs, short pieces by the great classical violinist and composer Kreisler; we worked on the Mendelssohn Violin Concerto, and lots more. I listened to a lot of classical music around that time. I was immersed equally in classical and jazz. During the day I'd play jazz in my classes with Marshall and at night I'd listen to classical music either in my dormitory or up the road in the auditorium when a classical concert was happening. I loved listening to Beethoven, Brahms, Bach and all the other composers who were floating through the mountain air. Someday I may record an album called "Bach, Ballads and Blues," an idea I came up with while I was in high school.

One time during one of our lessons, I was working on a particularly frustrating passage, the opening of the Mendelssohn. It is so slow and beautiful and you have to play it with just enough feeling and gentleness. You can't overdo it at all, but you have to make it sing. It's a very tricky balance. I was whining and complaining for about the millionth time and saying I couldn't do it when she actually slapped me in the face. I was shocked. I began to cry and I think she did too, but I understood. There's no time for whining if you're going to play the violin.

Finally, after months of work with Dima and the creative guidance from Marshall, I was able to start sculpting my vision for myself and for my life. I will never forget the patience and the generosity that these two people have shown me, not only throughout our years of friendship, but especially in the first weeks and months of knowing them. Without either of them, I don't think I would be playing today.

I was likely half way through my first year as a junior at Idyllwild, and I was firmly committed to not quitting the violin and to continue playing jazz. I needed to get several people's permission if I wanted to change my major, and although Marshall wanted me in his program and I wanted to be in it too, it unfortunately wasn't our decision alone to make. So, I set up a meeting with the Dean of the Arts and the Dean of Music to discuss my newfound purpose.

The Dean of the Arts was somewhat supportive, but cautioned me against changing my major because he said that the jazz program was not an easy program to switch into, that I'd "have to get my chops together" (a phrase I had never heard before, but meant that I'd have to be able to play well) and that it would be a big hassle with the paperwork. I knew right away that these reasons weren't really reasons. I think I started to cry.

The meeting with the Dean of Music was even worse. He said some of the most false, discouraging, close-minded things I've ever heard about music in my life. He told me there was a reason that nobody in the world played jazz violin, that nobody had ever done it before at the school and that nobody could teach me, that if I chose this major I would have no future, that there would be no place to study jazz violin after high school, and that allowing me to study it would reflect badly on Idyllwild Arts Academy, that is if I were to graduate at all.

I didn't cry that time, but as soon as the door shut behind me I did. Also, he had a sign on his door for a while that said, "Just because you're unique doesn't mean you're useful." That phrase may be true, but it isn't a very positive or encouraging thing for the Dean of Music to have on his door at an arts high school. Unfortunately, it was the school's belief that changing majors is irresponsible and promotes indecisiveness and rewards students for a lack of dedication.

I think, however, that if you want to change your path you should have the freedom to change it! Many famous artists changed their minds before they became famous and it only made them stronger. Why not let teenagers run with a new idea? It seemed to me that this philosophy was both backwards and far too strict. It actually limited creative potential rather than focusing it. Of course there were people in my corner, faculty like Andrew Leeson and others that encouraged me to see the beauty and uniqueness in my playing. He helped me see how important it was that I follow through. I appreciated that, but no matter how good I thought I was or wasn't, I still needed to convince the school that this was the right thing to do.

So I left that meeting feeling like I would fail. I didn't know what to do. Without my parents involved in the situation at all to help the administration change their mind, I had nobody to back me up. Even worse, the Dean of the Arts had told me that if they did allow me to become a jazz violin major, it wouldn't be official until the start of my senior year, so I'd have to finish my junior year doing all of the work that the jazz majors did without getting any credit for it, then come back for my senior year and then I could be officially in the program. Well, it was a pain in my ass but that's what I did.

The Dean of Music, who knew nothing about jazz, finally decided to schedule an audition in Marshall's classroom in front of him and Marshall so that they could decide based on how I played if I was good enough. Marshall and I showed up at the scheduled time and waited for almost an entire hour but the Dean of Music never showed up. His office was only a pinecone throw away! I never found out why he didn't show up. I went home to my dorm and wondered what would happen. Later that night, I got a phone call from someone at the administration and I was granted permission to become the school's first jazz violin major starting the fall of 2008. I was so excited! I remember when I got the news I was sitting in Dima's room. I think I cried then too, this time tears of joy.

:| 5 |:

The Year That Followed

"Remember who you are and what you stand for."
— *Idyllwild Arts Academy Proverb*

In the spring semester of my junior year, Dima had decided to go to Juilliard in New York City for college so we were making the most of our last few months together before she went off to school. I remember the night she was sending the last bits of paperwork from California to New York. We were three hours ahead of New York and it had to be there by midnight and it was 8:50pm in California. We were running through the woods on campus trying to get a security guard to open one of the classrooms so we could fax this bloody thing. With only a minute or two to spare, it got there on time. That was a dramatic moment. It was like the end of a "Mission Impossible" movie. We were staring at the clock, then at the fax machine, then back at the clock, then back at the fax machine. It was hilarious! They took her application thank *goodness*.

During the last few months of that year before she went to New York and the school year ended, we got to play together with our friends on their jazz recitals and in some student film scores. I was busy playing in Marshall's shows while Dima was busy playing in the orchestra. We were just dreaming about the future. We told each other about the jobs and gigs that we were dying for a chance to play on. She always talked about how much she wanted to play in this symphony or that one, and I talked about wanting to play with people like John Mayer, Stevie Wonder, Prince and Wynton Marsalis. Not much has really changed!

The next fall came around and it was one of the best feelings of my life. It was 2008. I showed up to campus with my suitcase and my violin, ready to start playing in Marshall's concerts and eager to tell everyone about my new major. I dropped my things at my new dorm room and I went immediately to go see all of my friends from the year before, and to meet all of the new students who had just arrived. It was like heaven, once again! It was fall and the leaves were turning colors. It was warm outside, the sun was high in the sky, and everyone was waiting to see one another and to talk about what had happened over the summer.

That year was just incredible. I played so much! I got to become close friends with Casey Abrams, who was in the jazz program at the same time with me. He and I played on each other's senior recitals at the end of the year, which I will never forget. Marshall started having me on his gigs at a local restaurant called Café Aroma. At night he would sign me out of the dorms while everyone was in room study doing their schoolwork. I would go play standards with him and other musicians that he would hire like Bob Boss, the school's jazz guitar instructor. We'd stay late and have dinner and dessert. It was fantastic. Sometimes we left the mountain altogether and went to Palm Springs or Los Angeles to play. That year, I also got to perform with the Kronos Quartet when they visited the school, which was tremendous. It was a year of friendship.

Toward the end of the fall, I started looking at colleges. Dima called my room one night from New York and told me that she had just met Jonathan Batiste, a fantastic jazz pianist who was also studying at Juilliard. She invited me to come visit her in New York during fall break for Thanksgiving so that I could meet Jon, visit New York for the first time, see if I could find a college I liked, and spend some time with her. I eagerly booked a flight to New York as soon as possible.

Right when I landed, Dima took me straight from the airport to her apartment at Juilliard. She told me that we only had five minutes to get ready before we had to go to Dizzy's and see Jon play the midnight show with his band. It was about a 15 minute walk from Juilliard to Dizzy's. I barely had my dress zipped and my lipstick on. I was so tired from my long journey from Idyllwild to Manhattan, but we went anyway. As soon as we got in the elevator at Lincoln Center we went into the green room and she introduced me to Jon. I went up to him and gave him a big hug.

He hollered very loudly, full of affection and enthusiasm. I've always liked that about him. He's never afraid to express his emotions. He and I have been friends ever since that moment. I guess it was a connection made by the spirit of music.

As soon as the band started playing I couldn't believe it. I had never heard New Orleans jazz music before and it completely blew me away. The whole band was an explosion of swing and positive energy. The personal character coming out of each of the musicians was so inspiring! I especially remember Eddie Barbash wailing on his saxophone. It was glorious. I decided right then and there that I would come to New York for school and that I would play with Jon, so that's exactly what I did.

In that week, I visited Manhattan School of Music and The New School for Jazz and Contemporary Music. I also wished that I could have auditioned for The Juilliard School, but their rules are very strict and they would never let a jazz violinist into the program – maybe someday that will change.

The trip to New York was a lot of fun. It was cold, but I enjoyed walking around Manhattan and going to various places to hear music. I remember getting to see the great pianist Eric Lewis play at Cleopatra's Needle and meeting lots and lots of people. We ate pizza late at night on the floor of the Juilliard dormitories, we walked through Central Park several times, and I made friends with many of her fascinating and inspiring classmates. I had fallen in love with New York.

When I got back to Idyllwild, there was snow on the ground and a lot of ice on campus. When it snowed, it was one of the most beautiful natural scenes in the whole world. The huge hundred foot pine trees could hold tons and tons of snow and it would gently fall to the ground every so often. It was like living in a giant snow globe. You could look out of your bedroom window in the morning and see these great big forests of white and dark green, gently swaying in the cold air. It was a silent fairy tale.

The only thing that wasn't like a fairy tale was getting up early in the morning and going to class while there was ice on the hills of campus. Some mornings you had to put your backpack down on the top of the hill and just sit on it and ride it like a sled down to class. If you actually tried to walk on the ice at an angle like that, you were sure to fall down and you'd slide down anyway! We all fell on the ice at least once a week. It was both painful and hilarious. The huge snow covered trees majestically towered over us as we fell like a bunch of little gnomes, books flying through the air, on our way to our classes. It was hilarious. I am laughing as I think of it now!

Winter break had arrived soon after that, and this Christmas was especially fantastic because my roommate had invited me up to San Francisco to spend the holiday with her family in Kentfield. Her father was Ed Catmull, one of the founders of Pixar. Spending time at their beautiful house was fascinating and inspiring, and Ed is one of the most intelligent and kind people I've had the pleasure of knowing. It was a week of shopping, eating, watching late night movies, relaxing, wrapping and unwrapping presents, drinking eggnog and sleeping in. It was exactly what I needed.

When I came back to Idyllwild for the spring semester, I had gotten word that I had been accepted to The New School. Fantastic! They had given me a scholarship and I was on my way to living in New York.

I finished the year with my own jazz recital and the surprise honor of receiving the "Most Inspirational Jazz Student" award from Marshall. It was all hitting me that my time at Idyllwild had come to an end. Ed Catmull gave a wonderful speech at our graduation ceremony and it felt like the end of an era, at least for me. I had gotten to know hundreds of fantastic artists and teachers from all over the world and I had two full, productive years in this magical place. I felt nervous at times about the contrast I was about to face with my move to New York just around the corner.

:| 6 |:

New York New School

"If we all did the things we are capable of doing, we would literally astound ourselves."

— *Thomas Edison*

The summer flew by and when I arrived in New York to begin school, I again moved into a dormitory, this time in the lower east side of Manhattan. *Talk about contrast!* I was excited to experience New York's people, its energy, and its glorious hustle and bustle. The late summer was coming to an end. It was still warm outside; people were out shopping, walking their dogs and sitting at cafes. All the college students were busy moving in. I loved the spirit of it all and the idea of exploring the city, but I was already feeling nostalgic about the peacefulness and the sense of belonging that I knew in Idyllwild. Still, there was no time for any such emotions, as classes were beginning soon!

Before school was set to begin, I was just about to turn 18 and Dima and I spent a few days or so getting to know the city together. She took me to her favorite restaurants, we walked through the different neighborhoods in Manhattan, she took me to some shops and I got to know the train system. Jon had invited the two of us to record on one of his songs on my birthday, so I spent the evening with all of my favorite people in the recording studio. After that we went to an old legendary diner on the upper west side called Big Nick's. We all had cake and they sang "Happy Birthday" to me. It was wonderful! In that moment I thought that every night in New York would be that special, but things changed once school began. For example, during my first weekend in college, I got thrown out of a New York University dormitory for throwing up on a security guard's shoes in the lobby. It was after midnight and I could tell she was in no mood for this kind of crap. I also threw a pen in her face at the front desk. It wasn't my best moment.

The New School for Jazz and Contemporary Music was a converted office building with two floors dedicated to jazz. I felt quite boxed in and immediately missed Marshall. The lectures in Idyllwild were about timing, life, and nature, and the lectures in New York were about chord changes, scales, and how to create more dissonance. I thought to myself, "*More* dissonance? That's what this lecture is about? Not more creativity, not more beauty, but *more dissonance?*" I came to have these types of thoughts many times a day for the duration of the two years that I spent there. I thought that many of the musicians I was hearing would have enjoyed a career in chemistry or mathematics much more than one in music. The way they played, the way they acted, and the way they spoke about music sometimes wasn't very musical at all. It's a little bit strange to me that I spent two years in Idyllwild and I spent the same amount of time at The New School, and yet I hardly ever think about The New School, and Idyllwild crosses my mind on a daily basis. I guess our minds prioritize positivity. Thank goodness for that.

I loved hanging around all of the other types of creative people at The New School too. Fashion designers, writers, environmental scientists, painters, sculptors, 3D animators, graphic artists, installation artists, filmmakers, language studiers, advertisers, web developers, everyone all packed into a few blocks of Manhattan. It was astonishing. The hallways of the dormitories at about 2:45am were a combination of beer, pot, artists in their sweat pants, young DJs milling about in their designer sneakers, computer geniuses eating baguettes and working on their projects, sketch artists whose hands and faces were covered in charcoal, students watching YouTube videos on their computers and phones, some guy who was chest deep in a masking tape and wire contraption, you name it. It was artsy and I loved it.

Aside from my thoughts about the school, there were a few musicians I met there who really impressed me; some came from Texas or New Orleans or other places on the East Coast and some came from other parts of the world. There was always a lot to be heard and I'll admit I barely scratched the surface despite being out and about almost every night. There were some incredibly talented people at The New School and I suspect that many of them will go on to do extraordinary things.

My freshman year in New York was coming to an end, and my sophomore year came in what feels like the blink of an eye later. I decided to move to Washington Heights, way uptown on the west side of Manhattan, into a two-bedroom apartment with Dima. A lot of our friends were living up there in the same neighborhood and they mostly went to Juilliard or Manhattan School of Music. Our place was cheap, and right off the A train which went to Juilliard off 59th street and went to The New School off of West 4th so sometimes we rode to school together. Despite living with my best friend, it was one of the hardest years either of us had experienced yet. She and I were both having a difficult time at school in our own ways. She was overwhelmed with schoolwork at Juilliard and I was underwhelmed by the New School's idea of jazz.

I've always thought that the jazz "pundits" as well as many of today's jazz instructors don't truly know what the general public likes about jazz. Sure, they know all about what jazz critics and jazz instructors like and what jazz students like (or at least what they think they like), but I don't think that many of them truly understand what the general public would call a great jazz concert. I'm talking about playing for kids that live in rural parts of the country, kids from all over the world, elderly jazz lovers, classical musicians, athletes, lawyers, doctors, people from every continent, everyone. Jazz can and should be enjoyed by all of these people, not just a collection of historians and musicologists.

Well time was passing by. I was still hanging out with Jon and with lots of his friends almost every night and was always inspired seeing them play just as much as I had been that first night at Dizzy's. We played together from time to time which was always fantastic, but in the meantime Jon was coming to our apartment every other night at least, usually around 4 a.m. after his gigs. He'd just knock on the door, put his things down on the floor and sit at the table. Dima and I would attempt to cook something for him and sometimes we'd stay up and talk about how things were going for all of us. He'd always keep us up hours after we should have been sleeping. Some nights we just stayed up all night and then just took our showers and went back to school. Some nights I'd be fast asleep and he would creep into my room and do this horrifying ghostly thing and yell, "Antooonnniooo… Carlloooooosss….. JoBIIIIMMMM!!!" It was terrifying.

I was also going to see Dima whenever she had concerts at Carnegie Hall or at Juilliard, and really enjoyed watching and hearing her whenever I could. To get out of the mindset of what was going on at The New School, I would hang out with my friends that were in other majors and spent lots of time downtown, enjoying the city and having fun. I should have been practicing more, but could feel myself burning out as the days and weeks and months went on. The less I thought about the violin, the less I could feel the feeling of burning out. So I pretended I wasn't a violinist on some nights to avoid that altogether.

During that year, although it was a difficult one, I still remember having a lot of fun. One night Dima baked *two* cakes for Jon's surprise birthday at Juilliard since the first one "wasn't good enough" and she turned our kitchen into a frosting and flour coated baking show. I remember trying to cook macaroni and somehow setting it on fire and creating "macaroni flambé" in our little uptown apartment. I remember other times when she and I dressed up for Halloween in masquerade-like feathers and glitter and went down to the Blue Note jazz club for Jon's Halloween concert and seeing Mike Thurber, Jon's bass player for that evening, dressed in a white sheet for the whole gig and everyone else in the band dressed as ghost busters. That was pretty amazing, I must say.

We used to go down there pretty often to hear Roy Hargrove or Cassandra Wilson or whoever was playing. Usually we could get on the guest list, so whenever we both had a night off we would go there and get a little table and listen to the music over a piece of cake. I also remember that Dima and I played in one of Jon's music video shoots at The Blue Note for one of his songs that we had recorded a few months earlier. There was always something going on. I ended up doing a short recording session with Jon and some of our other musician friends at Juilliard that year as well. We recorded some standards in a large studio room at the school, and I remember it was a terribly rainy and cold day. I released those recordings on the Internet once I had moved to California, about a year or so later. It's amazing when you listen to old recordings of yourself how revealing they can be about your state of mind at the time of the recording session.

I always kept busy during the day with various work-study jobs at The New School so that I could have some spending money. I also took an internship in Marketing at EMI, which I really enjoyed. I got to learn all about how a major label is run and helped out with projects at Blue Note, Astralwerks, Virgin, Capitol, and a few other labels. When I wasn't there or at school, I was out hearing music or seeing friends.

I remember marching through the street all afternoon, playing and singing with Jon in his New Orleans style parades up in Harlem with Chuck Prevost and all of our friends and turning any soul food restaurant into a full on jam session. People stood on tables playing their instruments. The customers went with it. I remember staying up late at night at Juilliard practicing in the practice rooms with Dima, trying not to fall asleep as the night got heavier and heavier on our eyelids. We spent countless nights at different diners and there was one night in particular when one of Jon's bass players, Phil Kuehn, put a whole handful of chocolate frosted cake in my face. Everyone unfortunately got involved and it turned into a cake fight in the middle of Broadway.

I remember getting dressed up with Dima and going down to the Highline Ballroom to see McCoy Tyner and Tom Harrell and other great musicians play. There were nights at Rockwood Music Hall, nights in the West Village, nights at Sullivan Hall, nights at that old waffle place by the Blue Note or at Mamoun's where you could get falafel all night long, nights at the Jazz Museum in Harlem, nights at the Rubin Museum when Dima and I played with Jon during one of his showcases, a Valentine's date with Dima in the dessert aisle of Whole Foods, another Valentine's date at a tiny Italian restaurant where everyone was celebrating their 50th Valentine's Day and the two of us were alone, crying and eating our endive salads and holding hands. Everyone thought we were a lesbian couple.

Once when we were at the apartment I had to go to the Emergency Room because I was having horrible abdominal pain. It was very late at night and I was panicking so Dima came with me. We walked down the block and over to the hospital and they checked me into the pediatric wing because I was 19. They did lots of tests but mostly we slept there all night.

Finally the doctors told me that I had been partially allergic to something I had eaten and that I would be fine. We shivered in my room in the ER all night, left the hospital at 7am, got a coffee, walked home, Dima took a shower and then she went to go teach her lessons. I can't believe she went through all of that for me, but I'd do the same for her. In New York you have to be tough!

I remember my first New York Halloween when she and I dressed up as cave women and walked around the city in animal print tattered clothing that we made ourselves. That was something. The Halloween party was at the Bowery Hotel and these parties always had a way of bringing out the wild side of people. It was a riot.

We ate Cuban food, Turkish food, Thai food, visited ice cream trucks in the summer, walked across the Brooklyn Bridge and through countless train stations together. You were always rushing to meet people or waiting for people who were rushing to meet you. The one thing you needed was a comfortable pair of shoes.

Now it wasn't always so fun. Dima recently reminded me of this horrible time one Spring when she and I were living in our apartment in Washington Heights but had been away for about a week visiting Idyllwild. After we left Idyllwild we went to San Diego to stay at Bob's Boss' house and to have some time near the ocean before we flew back to New York. I was convinced that I was leaving New York as soon as the school year was through, and since we were more or less on spring break, I only had about six weeks left. I didn't want to go back to New York and I remember I procrastinated in getting my return plane ticket until the day we flew, or maybe the day before.

Dima, always knowing the right thing to do, convinced me to come back to New York with her. Together we went to San Diego airport and got on a plane to New York. I was supposed to be in class that day at The New School and remember at the airport that one of my professors called me on the phone and asked me where I was. I told him I was in California.

Finally we got back to New York, took the train 200 or so blocks all the way up to our apartment, walked up four flights of stairs with our bags, opened the door and our apartment was flooded. There we were with our luggage and the whole place was full of water. Dima told me that at this point she felt that the world had ended. We were starving so we walked down the street to eat some Chinese food, brushed our teeth and washed our faces in the bathroom at the restaurant and then went home.

Our landlord didn't feel like fixing the flood, but luckily, one way or another he finally did. I can remember so many times that we didn't have heat, hot water, electricity or Wi-Fi – one of those things was always on the fritz. One time I remember coming home and the glass window next to the buzzer was completely smashed, so anyone who wanted to come into the building could just put a hand through and buzz himself right up! It was like that for weeks. Our bathroom flooded a couple other times too – there was always something going on with the pipes or this or that. There were some friendly repairmen who came to fix things, but they always left an unbelievable mess. Our landlord told us one time he was going to kill us, straight to our faces. We moved out shortly after that.

Carl lived in New York for a short while also. He was staying in Brooklyn with a friend he had met in the city. During that time my second cousin from Spain called Lluis was in New York studying at New York Film Academy as well. I got to see them every so often, which was lovely. I wish I had seen Carl more when he was in town. We didn't see each other all that often because New York has a strange way of alienating you from people, even your loved ones. New York just sucks you into its drama and busy energy. It makes you a little more self absorbed and out-of-breath than most other cities do.

Earlier in the winter, I found out that one of my roommates from Idyllwild (the one who I had spent Christmas with), who at the time was attending New York University, had decided to go back to California to attend The University of Southern California in Los Angeles. Especially now, with the winter approaching, this looked very appealing to me. I re-searched the school and decided to take an audition for jazz. I flew into Los Angeles that winter and auditioned for the jazz program, and was pleased that many of the faculty members had heard of Idyllwild Arts Academy and some were even old friends of Marshall's. I was beginning to feel like myself again, right in the middle of that audition, even with all of my nerves. I remember I played "A Nightingale Sang in Berkeley Square," for the panel. Now *that's* a song.

:|| 7 ||:

California, Here I Come!

"Travel brings power and love back into your life."

— Rumi

I n the spring, I received a message notifying me of my acceptance and my scholarship to USC. Just as it was in Idyllwild, I was also the first person to major in jazz violin at USC. I was very sad to be leaving Dima in New York but she had many friends to keep her company once I left. It had been a tumultuous year for both of us, but after much deliberation, I knew that it was the right thing to do.

As I was walking out of the apartment with my suitcases, I couldn't help but to remember what Dima's mother had said to me a few years ago when I visited them in their apartment in Sofia, the capitol city of Bulgaria. Dima's mother is a brilliant, sweet, strong woman who I admire very much. As I was leaving their apartment in Bulgaria, her mother hugged me, looked right into my eyes and said to me in Bulgarian, "I hope that you achieve everything that you want to achieve." After Dima translated what she had said to me in English, I started to well up a little bit in the elevator on the way down. That was one of the nicest things anybody had ever said to me. As I left our apartment in New York and the door closed behind me, I pretended that Dima's mother was there, saying the same thing to me again.

∞

USC started in fall 2011, and I was very excited to begin the second half of my college education. There was more than enough to keep me occupied at school, but I spent most of my time exploring Los Angeles and playing as much as I could. I wanted to make up for lost time, so that's exactly what I did. I immediately recorded two albums featuring guitar and bass. The first one was called, "Let It Rip!" and the second, "Generation Gap."

One thing I really enjoyed about the university was the variety of classes one could take. This wasn't the case for a school like The New School, which was a conservatory with music classes only. At USC I took full advantage of the array of possible subjects to dive into so I could keep my mind sharp. I was a jazz major, so I was taking all sorts of music courses like theory and jazz piano and had a private lesson every week with the jazz guitarist Bruce Forman too. I took some courses in classical music history and music business as well as several dance classes, a course on emergency medicine, and I even got my Emergency Medical Technician (EMT-B) certification. I think in another universe I could have become a heart surgeon.

I also took science courses like Oceanography and Environmental Science and I studied Spanish for several semesters. I took writing courses, literature, several history courses, and even completed a semester long course on Jimi Hendrix which was incredibly fascinating.

In addition to its regular orchestra which I was not part of, USC also had an orchestra they called the Gala Orchestra which they used for popular music performances. I played in it on several occasions and we did shows with Arturo Sandoval, Kristin Chenoweth, Barry Manilow and Glenn Frey from The Eagles.

Once we played the NBC Holiday tree lighting special in Los Angeles and Barry Manilow was the featured guest with the orchestra. While the cameras were live, Barry was his usual "stage" self, but during the commercial breaks, when the cameras were off, he was hilarious! He sat at the piano and yelled at us, "What do you wanna hear?!" He immediately started playing the theme from *Copa Cabana*. It was amazing. He was full of energy and humor and I loved watching him off camera. They should have put *that* on TV!

In those years I was doing a lot of odd gigs. I was a background actress for TV movies, I played in soundtracks for student and independent films, played the occasional solo violin clip for the soundtrack to a western film or a primetime TV show, was on *Glee* for one episode, played in music videos for other bands, played with flamenco dancers and Irish rock bands, jazz groups, country artists, blues bands, rap artists, and just about any other kind of musical group you could imagine. I played a lot of private parties, too. There was Jewish music, classical music, jazz music, electronic music, Indian music, French music, and almost any other type of music. You name it and I probably tried it. I even found myself once in a Sushi Bar in Los Angeles playing Baroque music for a party of historically dressed pirates.

Some nights I found myself in bars, one or two o'clock a.m. making a little cash or sometimes just playing in exchange for a meal, surrounded by broken glass and a mess of patch cables on the floor, and I often had class at nine the next morning. It wasn't easy, but I was always grateful for the work and tried my best not to take it for granted even when I was falling asleep in my classes the day after.

Also at USC I had the lucky fortune of meeting another one of my closest friends, Michelle Amanda Tseng. Michelle was a senior when I was a junior and she studied classical violin with violinist and philanthropist Alice Schoenfeld.

Michelle and I happened to meet in the practice rooms late one night. I stumbled into her room where some other classical musicians were taking a break from practicing, and she and I got to talking. I immediately loved her easy-going, fun-loving personality. The first thing I observed about her was that she was the total opposite of a snob. She was completely uninterested in competing with others and had a very calm and welcoming demeanor. It didn't take long for us to become good friends.

For about a year, Michelle and I lived in the same building near the university. I loved getting through with a day of class or practice and meeting up with her to catch up and unwind. I don't know how many times she and I stayed up until three a.m. in one of our rooms talking about life, eating chips and salsa in our slippers, and drinking orange juice straight from the carton. We used to watch improv comedy on TV, did our laundry together, told each other about what was going on in school, ate lots of peanut butter cups, stayed up late in the practice rooms wreaking all kinds of havoc, listened to our favorite recordings, and occasionally we would catch the local basketball games downtown or on campus. It was a great time. Michelle also gave me occasional violin lessons and every so often we'd have a gig together on campus, usually recording music for the film school.

One year on my birthday, Michelle, Dima and I were all in Los Angeles at the same time. It was a miracle! We decided to go paddle boarding at the marina in the daytime. We all love the water and wanted to spend some time in the sun. I had gone paddle boarding before but the two of them hadn't, so I gave them a proud and pompous speech about how they might fall in the water and not to worry and so on. We got out on the water and we were all paddling around the marina and everything was going fine. I started heading towards a buoy, and thought if I just bent my knees enough and tapped it with the front of my board, nothing dramatic would happen.

Well, I tapped the front of the board alright and it made a loud noise like a gong. The whole board started to wobble, and I was running backwards like a lumberjack on a log! My paddle went flying off to the side. I went flying off of the board and into the water. It was quite a commotion. I was screaming like a maniac and had to grab Michelle's boyfriend Hans' leg so that he could pull me out of the water. The whole incident was quite unbelievable.

I saw one of the best concerts of my life with Michelle. We went to Disney Hall in Los Angeles to see Wynton Marsalis with the Jazz at Lincoln Center Orchestra. It completely blew me away, the way he played his horn like he was walking down the sidewalk, but in a concert hall! Man! He would just look at the audience, stand up, point his horn straight to the back of the hall and go. It was a vision. It was one of the most powerful musical performances I have ever witnessed. People were standing up cheering and whistling, and some were even dancing. I was crying tears of pure joy. It rivaled the first night I ever heard Jon Batiste back at Dizzy's in New York.

In 2012 I started to visit San Diego more often, and got to know dozens of musicians who lived and worked there. There was one in particular who would become one of my favorite young people to collaborate with and his name is Matt Hall. He played trombone and was in the Marine Corps band for several years. I later met a bassist called Will Pierce and pianist called Ed Kornhauser and over the weeks and months our group of friends got bigger and bigger. The jazz community in San Diego really surprised me. There were people young and old playing on a nightly basis all over the city.

While visiting San Diego I always liked to see my good friend Victor in Chula Vista when I could. Victor is about Marshall's age and the two of them go way, way back. Marshall introduced me to him back when I was in high school at Idyllwild Arts. Victor is a very tall African-American man. He is very gentle and slow moving and speaks with a low, patient voice.

He and his late wife Elizabeth always offered to let me stay at their house and they were exquisite company. They were great listeners and conversationalists and there was always food to eat. Their house was full of books and instruments and artwork, sometimes made by their own personal friends. They had a piano in the living room and a pool outside which overlooked a golf course and a tennis court. Marshall loved to swim laps in the pool and play tennis next door. They had a cat called "Misterioso," named after the composition written by Thelonious Monk.

I can remember on several occasions waking up to Marshall playing keyboard early in the morning downstairs. Marshall always liked to play a ballad or something totally improvised. His improvisations were always reminiscent of Duke Ellington or Ahmad Jamal. Misterioso was never far away from the music.

The first time I stayed at their house was in 2009. Marshall and I were performing in a summertime concert at a theater in San Diego. It was one of Marshall's Seahawk MOJO concerts, also known as the Seahawk Modern Jazz Orchestra. I've performed many times with Seahawk MOJO over the years. It's always a huge production involving a string section sometimes as big as an orchestra, an entire big band and lots of special guests ranging from poets to dancers to percussionists to instrumentalists to singers and anything in between, all celebrating the multi-cultural and multi-generational history of jazz.

This time, we were honoring Nelson Mandela and the featured soloists were me, Casey Abrams, Richie Cole, Gilbert Castellanos, Daniel Jackson, Joshua White, Harold Mason, Charlie Owens, Yve Evans, Bob

Boss, Marshall himself and many others. There were two other musicians I remember very fondly called Leland "Spoonful" Collins who played spoons and danced, and Danny "Slapjazz" Barber who specialized in jaw harp and body percussion, something he did with white golf gloves on. The saxophonist Charles McPherson was there that day too, but he was in the audience.

Unfortunately Elizabeth has since passed, but every time I see Victor he always has a wise and friendly thing to say to me. Victor has taught me many things about life as a musician and always speaks about his friends like Marshall and Daniel and others with so much respect and love. Victor has been a quiet but strong force in my life. Even in his elderly age he hasn't lost any of his passion for living life, for helping others, and for sharing profound thoughts. I have so appreciated his friendship and guidance and I hope that he knows just how loved he is.

When I found myself near San Diego and wasn't staying at Victor's in Chula Vista I would stay at Bob Boss' house, up the coast about an hour in Oceanside. There, I would always wake up to the sound of Bob playing guitar in his living room, which overlooked the Pacific Ocean in the distance. I just loved staying at his house. He and his wife Vicky had a beautiful garden, a fireplace, an amazing record collection and there was always very, *very* good coffee. I'm not much of a coffee connoisseur myself, but I just know it's true. Over the years their house has become the unspoken international headquarters for jazz musicians visiting San Diego.

A few years later I visited the Marine Corps Base at Camp Pendleton. I was hired to play in a concert for their annual 4th of July Celebration on the beach, playing violin with a country band for tens of thousands of Marines and their friends and families. After the show, I headed to the side of the stage to pack up my things. One of the higher ups gave me a special coin after the concert to thank me for playing. I remember I was wearing a red sundress and some tan boots that day. I didn't know anyone in the band very well and I had come to the concert alone. Aside from meeting some children who walked by the stage, I was keeping myself company until some marines walked up to me and struck up a conversation. I showed them the coin I had just gotten and we began to walk around the beach and got to know one another. It was really fascinating. I had other friends who had gone to war before, but it was a whole new experience meeting a group of veterans all at once. They all treated me very well despite having very crass senses of humor toward one another. They called me "miss" and "ma'am" and constantly made sure I was safe and comfortable.

There was one veteran from the Marines whom I became much closer with after meeting him that night at the concert. He and I kept in touch over the phone and I visited him several times at the base. He was a kind young man who had gone to the Marine Corps right after high school and had just finished a tour in Afghanistan. His family was far away on the East Coast and he didn't really have anyone nearby who wasn't in the military, so I liked that I could be a friend to him and someone that he trusted. He was patient, brave and compassionate, and could listen for hours. After that summer I entered my senior year of college as he was deployed a second time overseas. He luckily returned safely to San Diego many months later and we continued to be in touch.

Our conversations had a simplicity and purity that I didn't seem to have with anyone else. He was interested in my life and I was interested in his. Although he never went to college and was a couple of years younger than me, he seemed to have this calm, mature demeanor that always made me feel very safe around him. Obviously going to war changes a person. I hope that someday, nobody in the world ever has to experience the senseless horrors and tragedy of war.

Somehow, despite all of that violence and isolation, he came out of it all with an unusual sense of peace and humility. He didn't seem interested in getting into fistfights or bragging about close calls in the desert. In fact, he didn't believe that war could solve any of the world's problems. He just wanted to be there to help as many people as possible. He wanted to make it better for them, not for himself.

Despite being deeply affected by the trauma and psychological burden of the war, something about him couldn't be upset. He was just too sturdy and resilient to be ruined, even by surviving in a war, *twice.* I consider him a personal hero of mine. He has since moved away from San Diego and started a family, but I think of him often and hope that he knows that's he's a hero to more people than just me.

My experience playing at the base made me realize how fulfilling and important it is to play for veterans and it's something I hope to do more of in the future. In 2015 I played as a guest with Clayton Cameron and his band at the Veterans Hospital in Los Angeles. We were outdoors celebrating Veterans Day, playing jazz for men and women of all ages and cultures. It was a beautiful day. Clayton's entire band was stellar and I got to play a bit with the great bassist Rickey Minor as well as a wonderful young singer Teira Church who were also guests of his. I know the Veterans loved the music, too. They were dancing and singing and clapping, and we got to meet many of them after the concert.

That reminded me of when I was a kid living in Madison. I used to play at the local nursing home several times a year. It's so important to share music and art with these people – people in hospitals, in nursing homes, people who have put their lives on the line for us. Art is truly one of the most uplifting powers humanity has to offer. We must all dedicate time to sharing music and art with as many people as possible, not always on a big stage and in order to make money, but sometimes for an even greater purpose, which is to thank others and to make them feel included and loved. This has always been one of my principle goals in making music.

:|| 8 ||:

Whirlwind

"You're supposed to be the leading lady of your own life,
for god's sake!"

– The Holiday

The year after graduation was one of the most adventurous years of my life. I went on many new trips, made some fabulous friends and grew accustomed to a new range of cultures and musical styles. Let me give you an example. Right out of school I went on tour as a soloist with Devi Sri Prasad, or as his fans know him, DSP. He's one of the most awarded film composers and pop musicians in India. Nearly all of the dancers, musicians and singers were from India, specifically, Chennai. There were only about five of us in a group of fifty or so on this tour that weren't Indian. The show was huge and we played it for tens of thousands of screaming Indian fans in arenas throughout the United States.

I loved learning about the way these musicians notated rhythms and chords and song forms. The percussionists were really inspiring in particular. They travel with cases and cases of different types of drums to feature during the show. The way that they play together in such relaxed but intricate rhythms was totally mesmerizing. It made me want to dance all night, and from the side of the stage, I did! Sometimes they invited everyone who performed in the show to come on stage to dance for one final number, so of course I could never turn that down. It was a party of lights, colors, flames, rhythms, dancers, singers, musicians, humor, and lot of love.

After one of the shows with DSP, I took a red eye back to Los Angeles and went straight from the plane in the early morning to Burbank. I had a meeting with Scott Cowie, a hilarious radio host, singer, songwriter, guitar player, drummer, multi-instrumentalist, author and comedian from Scotland. He was staying with a friend in Los Angeles and asked me to come over to do some recording for a couple of his songs and to have an interview. Scott later had me on his weekly Talk Music Podcast for a second interview and he also managed to recruit me to be a part-time co-cost and a guest violinist. Each week he interviews a different musician or artist from somewhere in the world. The podcast just celebrated its 100th episode! It's amazing how connected the world of performers has become.

One thing I really love is running into fellow performers when one or both of you are traveling. It's very interesting. Everyone has their own thing when they are on the move – some wear the same clothes for days and days, going from airport to airport with a mini keyboard packed in their carry-on bag and headphones perpetually around their necks. Some people dress to the nine's and are always prepared to perform, always coming from or going to a gig or meeting. Some travel in sweat pants and sweatshirts on little to no sleep for many nights in a row, carry a special brand of candy in their pockets and wear sunglasses to keep a low profile. Everyone has his or her own thing, no matter the season, time of day or location in the world. You may see someone in London in the fall and then in Los Angeles in the spring and they'll be wearing the same clothes.

That same summer I played violin in a string quartet with Sam Smith at the MTV Video Music Awards in Los Angeles. That was a great performance because it was Sam's mainstream U.S debut. His performance was one of the favorites of the whole show as well, and I can see why. Sam has a tremendous voice and has clearly dedicated an enormous amount of time and focus to practicing and refining his talent. I know a few singers who could take a page out of that book!

2014 also brought my third album, "Little Dipper" to life. I remember the exact moment that it went live. I was on tour with DSP and we were in a parking lot in front of a very average looking hotel around 1 A.M. on a balmy evening in June. We all had our luggage and were coming back from a show. I was yelling in the middle of the parking lot, "My album is out! My album is out right now!" Everyone was looking at me like, "Move your damn suitcase," but I felt like I was on fire no matter who else knew it.

I had planned to record "Little Dipper" in one day in Los Angeles at a studio in North Hollywood. It was the spring, I was 22, and I was busy finishing off my final semester of college at USC. I had booked the studio and hired the band, which was me, a pianist, a drummer, and a bassist. We were set to rehearse for one day and to record the next. I showed up to rehearsal, we ran through the repertoire and although it wasn't as effortless as I had hoped it would be, I, at the time, thought that it was good enough to record.

After we finished the rehearsal and left, the pianist immediately called me and told me he didn't want to do the recording. He told me he thought he sounded terrible and didn't feel comfortable recording the material. Well I thought that he sounded really quite good, but I suppose he didn't feel right about it. So, as I was driving home, a sinking feeling came over me that this wasn't the right band. I began to have doubts about the other two musicians as well. I didn't doubt their musical ability or their personalities or anything. I just doubted them being right for this recording. After all, it's my damn recording. Now, looking back on it, I know that my doubts were not just anxiety or needless worry but my gut was telling me something. *This is not the way I am going to record this album.*

I sent a message to all of the band members telling them that the recording was off. I may have told them that there was something going on with the studio or there had been a mix up, but the truth was that I just didn't want to go ahead with the project like this. I had no plan except to cancel the date and to rectify my vision.

Luckily, the studio was extremely accommodating and allowed me to call off the session that was supposed to happen the following day. I rebooked the studio about a week or two later, hired three friends from San Diego (Ed Kornhauser, Will Pierce and Ryan Shaw), they all came up to Los Angeles the day of the session, and without a rehearsal we finished the whole thing in one day. It may seem a bit reckless to cancel a recording and to fire the whole band the day before it's supposed to happen, but here's something I learned; if you can dodge a bullet, dodge it! You'll be glad you did. Don't waste your energy. Do it right the first time, by any means necessary.

There's an art to picking the right musicians to record and perform with and everyone has their own method. Mine is to keep trying. It's trial and error by way of focusing in on what you want the band to sound like and then paying attention to which people most successfully pull that off while making whatever you're doing an enjoyable experience. When you find those people, never let them go!

In the fall of 2014 I was invited by Zane Carney to play as a special guest on one of his shows at Hotel Café in Hollywood. Zane is truly one of the greatest guitarists in the world. You'll just have to hear him sing and play to understand what I mean. Jon Batiste happened to be in town, so I introduced them before the show and brought Jon up on stage with me. The three of us played the jazz standard "Skylark" that night and brought the house down. I was beside Zane Carney and Jon Batiste on stage. It doesn't get much better than that!

Another one of my favorite parts of 2014 was traveling to Shetland, Scotland on one of Martin Taylor's guitar retreats. I met his whole family there and quickly became close with his daughter in law, Alison Burns. She is a fantastic jazz singer and a hilarious, spirited person. She makes things happen. She's a visionary with a lot of optimism and a hell of a work ethic and I really look up to her. Tommy Emmanuel was also there for part of the retreat and Martin, Tommy and I had a little jam session in The Lounge, one of the local pubs on the island. It was crowded with the local musicians and townspeople, totally packed until closing time. There were instruments lining the walls and all of the tables were covered in glasses. The tables were wooden and on the chairs and benches were piles of coats and mittens.

It was very cold and windy the whole time we were there, but I got used it. For a couple of the days, we had master classes from Martin and Tommy in a lighthouse on a hill. Up there we had a beautiful view of the waves breaking along the rocky shore. It was so windy coming down from the top of the hill that I almost blew off the cliff! My nickname for the whole week was "Wee Nora."

At the end of the week, Martin invited me up to play a tune with him in the Shetland International Guitar Festival. Many of the guitarists on the trip including Martin played on closing night, which was marvelous! Martin and I did a little tribute to Martin's work with Stéphane Grappelli and I really enjoyed that.

Martin brings out the best in people. He is such a warm and welcoming person, and is a fantastic teacher as well. Something I've really admired about his teaching is that he explains things in terms of bigger concepts rather than minute details. He is able to address a group of people with a wide range of musical abilities and they all finish the lecture feeling like they've been illuminated, myself included. He doesn't teach by confusing people or making them feel inadequate. Rather, he helps people to build on their strengths and their intuitive knowledge, which is why so many people from around the world love to learn from him. He can always find a way to make a person feel good right here and right now.

I love the way Martin tells stories as well, and he has so many! He's been playing guitar and performing for about 50 years, so you can always count on Martin telling a great story that will make you laugh. I also love the way he talks about the history of jazz. Once I remember he described the Quintet of the Hot Club of France (Stéphane Grappelli and Django Reinhardt's gypsy jazz band from Paris) as the ancestors of every European jazz musician.

Later on the same trip, I went to London and visited another new friend, saxophonist and composer John Altman. I remember going to his house and listening to dozens of jazz violinists that I hadn't even heard of on what I call his "Sofa of Knowledge." I'm not talking about the great jazz violinists like Stuff Smith (who invented the electric violin), Joe Venuti, Eddie South, Ray Nance and all of them. I'm talking about some really obscure geniuses! The history of jazz violin is so rich! It's unfortunately just not very well known, even to many jazz musicians. I'm not sure why most institutions don't teach the history of jazz violin like they do the history of jazz guitar and piano. There are violinists featured on all sorts of classic recordings from Duke Ellington and Oscar Peterson to Ella Fitzgerald and many others. It's just that most people wouldn't be able to name them.

In a sense, violin has a place in jazz as much or more so than almost any other instrument. The violin was used in African-American music long before the blues even existed, and it was around hundreds of years before the saxophone came along in the mid 1800's. The violin was one of the main instruments in early blues music (the music from which jazz evolved), and was central to old American folk music and what became known as "fiddle" music. That tradition of course evolved to country and western music.

The history of the violin itself dates back about 500 years in total. The first "modern" violin was created in the late 1600's or early 1700's in Italy, and it's changed little since then. So the history of violin can really be traced through many cultures and types of music over the last half millennia or so. It's a beautiful and fascinating history and I plan to help keep it going strong.

I continued to visit London several times over the next year and on my second trip, John had me up as a special guest on his show at Pizza Express in Soho. It was a tremendous honor to play there with John and the band. That night was also the first night I ever played with Jacob Collier. We played "I Got it Bad and That Ain't Good," as a duet. You wouldn't know it, but the first note we ever played together was the first note of that duet in the show. There was no rehearsal, no nothing. Everyone loved it. Jacob is a wonderful musician, and one of the most internally honest people I know. It's almost as if he is immune to outside negativity. He always has an answer to every question and uncertainty, even if the answer is, "I don't know yet." One of the best things he ever told me was, "You've just got to figure out what your vibe is and just be in that." He's always creating and constructing his own world wherever he goes, whether it's at home in his music room or on stage somewhere far away.

He, more than anyone else I know, understands the importance of feeling comfortable with yourself and the limitless effect that being comfortable has on music. He always has a kind and encouraging word to say to his fans and friends. Everyone knows that he's a musical genius, but what some people don't realize until meeting him is that he is also a very insightful and warm inspirer, a true one-of-a-kind.

On that same trip to London I played with two great guitarists, Jim Mullen and Larry Coryell. Larry invited me to sit in during his show at Pizza Express, which was a lot of fun. I didn't know what we were going to play when I walked on stage, but after playing a little bit of jazz we ended up doing a full blown tribute to Cream's bassist, Jack Bruce. It was a sold out show and Larry really put me out in front! These are the moments that make you grow as a musician.

After that, Pizza Express offered me my own show. I was really excited to make this my first true solo debut in the UK. I was also asked by LivAmp to live stream it around the world. Pizza Express had never live streamed a show before so we made history that night. I was also very happy with my band for that evening. There wasn't a rehearsal. All we had was a sound check. I met most of them for the first time during that sound check and then we all played together for the first time that evening. When you have a show that starts in two hours and you have to organize and rehearse a two-set show in 45 minutes (and memorize everyone's name too!), there's no time to dillydally.

When you have great musicians, things just come together. I was lucky enough to have some friends in London who referred these musicians to me and *man, were they on point!* Terry Gregory who was an old friend of Stéphane Grappelli's played bass, Rob Luft played guitar, Dave Newton played piano, Lloyd Haines played drums and I had John Altman on saxophone and Alison Burns singing as special guests. An added bonus was that we reached people all over the world through the live stream. Over ten countries tuned in!

I finished off that London trip sitting in with the great guitarist John Etheridge at a Hampstead house party and a performance with Martin Taylor during the City of London Festival. The party with John Etheridge was really special because it was a fundraiser for a wonderful charity called Animals Asia. I love to play for charities and it's always great to play for people who you wouldn't normally have the chance to play for.

The performance with Martin was wonderful, as well. I played with him as a special guest in an old masonic temple in the middle of the city. The inside of the temple was lined with different shades of teal, cream and black marble. It had beautiful architectural details and artwork along the walls and ceiling. Even the floor was decorated. Martin's whole family was there that day and I love it when I get to see them! Alison was a special guest on the show as well. The three of us make a fine team if you ask me!

Before I came out to play, Martin introduced me by telling the audience that he hadn't really worked with another violinist since Stéphane Grappelli, not until I came along. That made me feel really appreciated and honored. It's great to be able to pass on their remarkable music now nearly 20 years after Stéphane passed away in 1997.

Aside from traveling, 2014 was also a year for making a lot of new friends in Los Angeles. I became friends with Clayton Cameron, a fantastic drummer who played with Tony Bennett, Sammy Davis Jr. and John

Mayer. I first met Clayton at Catalina's jazz club while he was playing with Kenny Burrell. I contacted him saying that I'd love to come meet him and he was nice enough to put me on the guest list for one of their shows. He stayed long after the show was over and all of the chairs were put on top of the tables. He told stories about what he was doing when he was my age and about all of his unbelievable experiences in New York and on tour. I love hearing about these stories, especially one-on-one. Clayton and I talked for a long time over cocktails about his days with Sammy Davis Jr. He told me about meeting Miles Davis, about getting his gig with Tony Bennett, and he also shared with me his admiration and enthusiasm for Sammy's talents.

In addition to being a great storyteller and someone with a fantastic memory, Clayton is one of the most spirited and positive musicians I've ever met. He's even played with me at Seven Grand. Thank goodness there are still many people like Clayton who are still around, people who are one or two generations removed from the great musicians from the 1960's. They can tell us all about our musical heroes and what it was like to learn from them, something I believe is an extremely precious resource.

One night, Clayton and me and some of our friends all went to a diner in Hollywood late at night after hearing Zane Carney play a show. Clayton talked to me for a long time about rhythms. I remember he sketched some rhythmic ideas and equations onto a napkin and gave them to me to study. You really never know when you're going to be given a valuable piece of information, and sometimes it comes at 2 a.m. on a napkin!

I also became friends with Morris Hayes, a keyboard player who was Prince's Musical Director for twenty years. Morris is such a generous and kind-hearted spirit. He thinks big and he is always coming up with new ways to bring ideas and people together to enrich a community. He's very inventive but still incredibly humble and receptive. He's always got an ear to the ground and is curious about what young people are doing in music. He's given me a lot of encouragement and helped me a long way toward building up my confidence. There's something he says that always makes me laugh. When he really likes what someone is doing, he'll say, "That was *severe*."

Another one of my new friends was Bobby "Hurricane" Spencer. Bobby is a fantastic blues saxophonist who has shown me nothing but love, encouragement, good humor, and a lot of great blues licks. Bobby's friends and family are all community loving people with strong enthusiasm for music. I am honored to know all of them. They welcomed me with open arms, fiddle and all! I also got to know Ray Goren, one of my favorite young blues guitar players, who will no doubt go on to do tremendous things. Of course, I can't forget Lester Lands, another amazing blues guitarist and singer from Louisiana. Lester introduced me to Bobby after Lester and I played together at Seven Grand, one of the places Lester's band and my band have been playing regularly for years. He is one of the most optimistic and genuine people I know. He can play and sing the crap out of the blues and still leave you smiling. I don't know how he does it.

It's important to keep friends around who you respect and admire. Don't keep a friend around if there's not much you respect and admire about that person. I always remember this: Show me your friends and I'll show you your future. Or, here's the way Oprah said it, "Surround yourself only with people who are going to take you higher."

After college I lived in a little studio apartment on Cherokee Avenue in Hollywood. I would often stop by the old Italian restaurant Miceli's to sit in with a pianist called Brian O'Rourke. Miceli's was barely two blocks away from my apartment and since Brian would play there four or so nights a week, I'd go meet him on my way home after my gigs. There we were, just the two of us, at 10 or 11 o'clock at night, playing standards. Playing with Brian was one of the greatest educations I have ever gotten, and he is one of my favorite living jazz pianists.

He had stories about anyone you could possibly mention, and he could take nearly any request as long as it came out before 1990. Aside from his incredible stride piano technique and timeless, flawless style he could also do things like play in different time signatures or key signatures with the right and left hand. In fact he could play totally different songs altogether with the right and left hand! It was something else. I would walk in there and have a little dinner or dessert and then we'd play together until the restaurant closed. We played ballads, jazz standards, the blues, rhythm changes, the occasional show tune, and themes from musicals and movies.

Sometimes there were many people there and sometimes there were only a few. It was an atmosphere, that's for sure. Everything in the restaurant was either wooden, green, or red. There were hundreds of empty Chianti bottles hanging from the ceiling and when we weren't playing, old recordings of Nat King Cole or Frank Sinatra filled the air. Brian was always really kind to me and told me many times after I played, "You're a tremendous talent." He always had a joke to tell, one that you had never heard before. It was amazing.

Then 2015 came to do its number on me. As a sort of follow up to my trip to Shetland, I got to see Tommy Emmanuel again, which is always a pleasure. He invited me to be a special guest with him in one of his shows in Los Angeles. Tommy always plays like it's the last time he'll ever play, and he can play all night, all day, and all night again. He has an unbelievable amount of natural energy and he's never afraid to *go for it!* He is not only a brilliant musician and performer, but an incredible friend and mentor, the kind I hope to become. Written in Sharpie marker on his guitar are some Beatles lyrics that say, "Life is very short and there's no time for fussin' & fightin' my friends!" *Man!*

Tommy has been a mentor to me mostly from afar. I don't know him all that well, but in the time I've spent and played with him I've learned a lot about generosity, stage presence, pre-gig preparation, how to greet strangers, how to behave at a jam session, how to tell a great joke, how to stay in touch with your family when you're on the road and far away from them, and all sorts of other stuff. There's a lot I admire and have picked up from him.

That reminds me of something. We should never play like we've got another chance to play. If we always take it for granted, the audience will feel like they've been taken for granted, too. We've got to pick up our instruments like it's the last time we'll ever get to and really focus on sounding the best that we can! That's the only way we ever will! There are times when the circumstances are not ideal, and in those times there's a choice to be made. But if we can learn to play our absolute best when it's not ideal, think about how much better we'll sound when it *is ideal* because we'll have trained to always play our best! We all must be prepared to play, to really get out there and do it.

After spending a little time in London with Jacob Collier and hanging out with his friends Louis Cole and Genevieve Artadi who were also visiting London from Los Angeles, Louis and Genevieve asked me if I'd move into a house with them shortly after we all got back from our trips.

In the spring of 2015, Louis, Genevieve another friend of Genevieve's called Alex and me all moved into a beautiful house in the hills above Downtown Los Angeles, near Highland Park. All of the best musicians in town came to visit. We had house parties and jam sessions nearly every week going until sunrise! I remember one night in particular when Jacob was visiting Los Angeles from London and he and I played ballads in the living room until seven a.m.

The parties at our house were a great way to meet people. Musicians from all over the world would wind up just walking through the front door. But we went out a lot too! I remember one time when Genevieve and I went to see Becca Stevens play. Billy Childs was there too, so after Becca's show, we went out to a diner in Hollywood and we all sat in a booth with Billy as he told us story after story about his life in music. He told us about being on gigs with this legend and that legend, about living in New York with Clayton Cameron and all sorts of other stuff. It was like a jazz history lesson, but it all happened over french fries and coffee.

Genevieve quickly became one of my closest friends and a huge inspiration to me. She's a world-class singer and an amazing songwriter, but I admire her character too. She taught me the importance of believing in your own taste and vision and not always leaving it up to someone else to tell you what the best way is. She also taught me about natural beauty. She helped me to understand that sometimes not wearing makeup is just as beautiful as wearing it. She also reminds me every day that it's important to embrace yourself in all your weirdness and uniqueness. I remember this especially when I see her perform or leave the house in a wacky yet brilliant outfit that only she could own, or when she comes back from salon with a totally new hair color. She is someone who lives in the moment, someone who hardly ever, *ever* complains. Plus, she knew how to shoot tequila. That -- we had in common.

One Halloween night she wasn't feeling very well. While there was a party going on downstairs at our house, she and I were upstairs in my room and she was lying in my bed wearing the better part of a skimpy Jane from Tarzan costume. I was wearing my spandex superhero outfit complete with a cape while she ordered me to sit down next to the bed and sing the ballad, "Secret Love" and accompany myself on the violin over and over and over again. It was a bit absurd, but she said it made her feel better. I must have played it 20 times. That's how I know if Genevieve is really not feeling well. I ask her, "Gigi, is it bad, or is it *Secret Love* bad?"

When I look back on my time at the house with Alex, Genevieve and Louis, I think I'll remember it as one of the best periods of my life. Aside from all of the parties and constant jam sessions, there is something special about this place. Maybe it's the way the sun comes up behind the hill, or all of the trees and flowers surrounding our house, or how quiet it gets at nighttime. Maybe it's the fact that we have an organ, a piano, a drum set, most of a recording studio in our garage that Louis built, about a dozen keyboards and a dozen more amplifiers to play with. Maybe it's the fact that someone is always singing jazz in the living room or dancing on the couch or telling a joke in the kitchen, or that if you are up and wanting a snack four a.m. there's always someone to hang out with you. Maybe it's the fact that someone is always doing something creative in the house like writing a song, shooting a music video or dreaming up a new idea. Even with all of the fighting and drama and the crying and getting to know one another, it's a dream. I feel that I can say or do anything and these people will love me anyway.

The amount of idealist creative freedom and raw uninhibited personality in this house is just amazing. To my left at this moment we have a life-size storm trooper balloon sitting on the bench and to my right in the kitchen is jar of pickles, a bottle of tequila and some friends are over composing on the piano. It's like this nearly every minute of every day. I wouldn't trade it for anything. We all inspire one another and confide in one another. We play on each other's recordings and gigs. It's like a hippy commune. It's a bohemian dream.

Now don't even get me started on Louis and Genevieve. They are two of the craziest people I have ever met! Together they make music in their band called Knower, whose music is explosive and contagious and has influenced a lot of musicians around the world including me. But separately they are something else too. Louis is one of the most witty, quick-thinking and totally un-self-conscious people I know. He is a true individual in every sense of the word. He doesn't go along with any idea he isn't wild about himself. That goes for clothing, the kind of music he makes, what he eats, how he spends his time, the opinions he has and just about anything else. Aside from being a musical genius songwriter and drummer, he will make a joke about anything you are talking about faster than you can realize he made one. He's also an honest and genuine person, someone who cares deeply for others and knows how to tell the truth in a loving way.

Genevieve is a fierce empathizer, always able to see the best in someone, always reminding people of their strengths and capabilities. Louis does that too. I feel incredibly lucky to spend as much time with them as I do. Hardly anyone can match their work ethic, their level of integrity or their ability to make friends with just about anyone. They have taught me the art of the 24-hour, 7-day-a-week work schedule with many naps and social events in between. It's really something. I wish everybody got the chance to live in a place like this, a bona fide "casa del arte" in the hills. Any house or apartment can be like this. All you have to do is get the right people together, add some sequins, a little creativity, an espresso machine, and voila!

Our house has a deck and when I go out at night I can see the beautiful stars and planets and galaxies and the "star stuff," as Neil deGrasse Tyson calls it, that we are all made of. This gives me great peace and a sense of belonging in the universe(s). Neil also reminds us that we are not just in the universe, but the universe is in *us!* One more incredibly poetic but scientifically accurate statement about human life comes from the scientist Michelle Thaller, who explains that because all of the elements that make up our bodies were created inside of stars that eventually burned out millions or billions of years ago or exploded into Supernovas, "We are dead stars looking back up at the sky." Sometimes I think about this when I'm on the porch at our house.

The third Martin Taylor Guitar Retreat that I attended was in the Amalfi Coast of Italy, just south of Naples. I loved being on the Mediterranean Sea, exploring the town of Atrani and walking along the nearby beaches. Martin's son James and his wife Alison were there again, and I got to see some old and new friends who had made the journey from all over the world. People came from places like Australia, the U.K., the U.S., Europe and beyond. Here we all were together. It was great!

We had a lot of fun in that week eating pesto, drinking Aperol Spritzes and going on boat rides up and down the coast. The water was crystal teal/blue and the scenery was spectacular. I loved all of the art, the jewelry and clothing. Alison and I had a fabulous time exploring all of the old-world peacefulness that Atrani provided and we told jokes and sang songs everywhere we walked. The way the town is decorated with little tiles and pottery and details is just breathtaking. We had jam sessions by the sea until about 3 a.m., saw some absolutely stunning fireworks on the roof of our hotel, and swam almost every day.

The Amalfi coast is lined with caves that are dark inside, but the way the sunlight comes in from the outside makes the water glow and shimmer the brightest blue you've ever seen. If you swim outside of the caves and look up, you'll see cliffs hundreds of feet high covered in grape vines, trees and little Mediterranean houses. In the town of Atrani the houses are all different colors and they're tucked away among little shops and churches in the hills. When you walk through the town there are many little stone passageways, steps leading left and right, up and down, and you'll pass by clothing lines where people's laundry is drying after a hard day's work.

I loved the food the most. We ate tons of pizza, olives, watermelon, pasta, eggplant and other Italian specialties. We also drank a lot of wine and there was always dessert. Gelato was my favorite. My trip to Italy may have been the best trip I've ever taken. It's a magical place with so much history and such a rich culture. If I ever go missing, Atrani will be a good place to start looking for me.

:‖ 9 ‖:

Finding Your Sound

"Creativity takes courage."

– Henri Matisse

Marshall used to talk to us in his classes about finding a sound, explaining that it's perhaps the most important task that a musician has in life. Without your own sound, you are just a technician. You're a player who has either taken on someone else's sound in an effort to duplicate or reproduce it, or a player who hasn't taken on any distinguishing sound or character and thus has no real defining qualities.

Just to be clear, I'm not talking about adding a drummer or taking away a drummer, or recording fast or slow music. The instrumentation and the style of what you're doing may change and it's supposed to change. That's called evolution. What I am talking about is the deeper concept of your individual sound. I'm talking about something that is deeper than just the sound of your instrument, the way society has heard it over and over, or the sound of the style of music you are playing. Your sound as a musician can be compared to the way you speak. When you speak, whether you're reciting poetry, reading the newspaper, talking to a friend or ordering a pizza, your voice is your voice. It shines through no matter what you're talking about.

I'm not sure why this is, but during one of Marshall's classes I can remember him saying, "Some of you will take a while to find your own sound and that is natural… it takes exploration and time. Some of you may have already formed your own distinguishing sound, like Nora.

Nora has her own sound." When he said this, I couldn't have been older than 17. And even more than that, I had only been playing jazz for about a year. I wasn't a prodigy or a genius at learning music or anything, so it really struck me that he singled me out. I gave it some more thought and wondered what goes into creating your own sound and making other people hear it the way you want it to come out. This is something that I will probably be working on for the rest of my life.

Firstly, it all goes back to what I was talking about the first day I ever played a note for Marshall, which was the first day I played a note of any real jazz, actually. I was sight reading ballads and slowly embellishing them based on the phrasing of the melody. I was using the emotion of the lyrics or at least of the notes of the melody themselves, without regard for the words, and using the gaps in between the phrases to add some connective material, the way an artist paints a patch of blue sky in between two green leaves.

So, my sound came out of experimentation with the melody. That, for me, is the basis for improvising at any tempo, in any style. You see it all over the musical world, in everything from Bach to fiddle tunes to rock to funk to jazz. Marshall was able to help me cultivate my own sound fairly quickly because of four things. Firstly, I had a desire to find my own sound (my musical speaking voice on the violin) and to find my own sound in the context of jazz; secondly, I was in an environment that was encouraging and I had a teacher who was willing to help me on my own personal journey and not just through my journey of 32 bars of chords; thirdly, my teacher, Marshall, understood the importance of building a personal relationship with his students and of being a good listener because he knew that by doing that, we would tell him what we needed from him in terms of guidance, musical, spiritual or otherwise; and finally, I was never taught to play in a mechanical way based on scales and chords, and I was never scolded for playing what's known as a "clam" or a wrong note. Marshall said there are no wrong notes; only "undesirable" ones. Sometimes the undesirable notes are a question of not what, but *when* as well.

Aside from those four principles, the student's desire to be great in whatever he or she is trying to do, encouragement from a teacher that addresses more than just music, listening by the teacher to the student in order to know what the students' needs are both in the moment and in a broad sense, and being taught naturally rather than mechanically, Marshall also knew when and how to challenge us. He wasn't afraid to see us fail as long as he knew that we could handle it. He was like some people's view of god in a sense, a god who gives you only tasks that he *knows* you are capable of succeeding in. Sometimes he let us fail not so that he could prove us wrong and gloat, but because he knew that we were young and could only learn certain lessons by going through them and seeing the truth in them from our own two eyes.

I'll use a metaphor, but pretend I'm talking about music. We would ask him to throw us a big boulder that he knew we couldn't catch. He'd say no. That's too big. We'd say, "Yes! Throw me the boulder!" He would throw it and it would almost always squash us. He would watch us throw boulders to one another all the time, but instead of laughing at us or telling us we couldn't do it, he'd keep his eyes wide open and his mouth shut, always waiting to see if someone managed to actually catch the boulder. I did that a few times, and even I surprised myself when I did.

A musical boulder could be anything from a song that was too deep and emotional for any 16-year-old to understand, transposing a song into a new key that was far too hard to play perfectly the first time, a tempo that was too fast or too slow to keep steady or something else.

I feel that a lot of young musicians miss out on this kind of training, which is a real shame. Not everyone can be taught by someone like Marshall. Some people are totally self-taught from the beginning and I think that's fantastic too. However, I do think it's important to remember that even if you are teaching yourself how to play, you must cultivate your own sound. You can be your own Marshall no matter what your age is. Be enthusiastic about what you're doing. Encourage yourself in more ways than just musical ways. Listen to what you need from yourself and from the world around you. And finally, give yourself the time, the space and the love to naturally evolve and don't scold yourself when you make a mistake. If you do those things, you'll find your own sound.

You can never seek it outside of yourself. You'll never find it anywhere else but within, and you already have it there waiting for you. You have to go deep to find it, and you can't be afraid of what anyone will think about it, either. I've had a lot of teachers that in every lesson only gave me more reasons to fear what people will think of me and my talent when I play, and that's no way to teach. That's no way to play! They want less intuition, and more thinking. One time I was even thrown out of a jazz ensemble at USC for "playing too much blues." Unbelievable. It's so demoralizing the way some teachers advise their students. Of course you'll quit if you have a teacher like that. How are you supposed to learn anything if the person you're meant to look up to doesn't inspire you?

When I was a kid I remember I liked to play by myself more than I liked to play with a group. Playing alone gave me the freedom to change the melodies of the repertoire without permission. I liked to add harmonies on the fly, or sometimes do goofy things like play the whole piece using just one finger on my left hand! When I was 12 or so, I remember playing a classical violin piece with my Japanese friend Ami, who had been a student of my mother's. We were performing together at a local school. In the rehearsal beforehand, when the end of the piece came around, I added an alternate ending that sounded like it was the end of an electrifying fiddle tune! It gave the piece that bit of the fire that I thought it so desperately needed. I taught it to Ami and we played it that way in the show. It was fantastic! That was one of the first times I tried arranging music and it just stuck. That's what finding your own sound is all about; questioning the mundane, making something your own, trying something you've never done before. It's all part of your evolution.

I was never afraid of was asking, "Why?" It got me in trouble sometimes, especially in my college years. Most of the professors at my schools (and I've found this to be true at other schools too) wanted the students to ask questions only as long as they were based in a context of the student believing that the professor knew the answer and that the professor's answer would be the right one. For example, professors liked questions like, "Could you explain your method of arranging this section of your award winning song to me?"

What they didn't like was students asking questions like the ones I sometimes asked. I wanted to know the purpose of what my professors were teaching me. I wanted to know their ideas about what it means to take a solo. I wanted to know how they felt their attitudes as teachers and the attitude of the school were contributing to individual creative expression.

They asked me to meet with them where they called me arrogant and disrespectful of authority, which were not true. To be honest, I thought that they were arrogant and disrespectful of students. They tried to get me to believe that I was unfit to be taught, I was behind the other students musically, and didn't fit their mission as a school. They didn't fit their own mission as a school!

None of the teachers or students defended me, which I thought was both selfish and weak. I didn't tell many people what was happening, mostly because I was afraid that they wouldn't take my side. I didn't want to give people reasons to dislike me even though I knew that there were several professors and many students who agreed with just about everything I was saying.

Plato couldn't have explained it better when he said, "Do not train a child to learn by force or harshness; but direct them to it by what amuses their minds, so that you may be better able to discover with accuracy the peculiar bent of the genius of each."

I think that many professors feel insecure about their lives or careers. This causes them to want to feel needed, like they are the fountains of answers. The students need to come to them with *the question* and they provide *the solution*. Well, that's not art. That's math. There's no freedom in that, and I wanted more freedom. I didn't want to be judged based on one person's opinion or style. I wanted my professors to trust me and to trust my own development. I seldom found anyone besides Marshall who did that.

I wanted to trust my professors too. I feared them taking away the very thing that made me *me* – you know, all of the stuff besides the notes like work ethic, vision, passion, optimism, creative confidence, the feeling of gratitude and of believing in the process. Many professors wear these qualities down in their students, sometimes without knowing it. It's not all about the notes. In fact, it's not about the notes *at all*. Without all that other stuff I just mentioned (and more), the notes will never, *ever* come out right.

Another thing that will make the notes come out wrong is fear. I try not to make decisions based in fear. If I worry about whether or not someone will like what I play or how I play it, and then I change what I'm doing because my ideas are now based in fear of audience reaction or fear of judgment, then the whole thing is backwards. The audience is there to listen to me. I am not there to listen to the audience. There of course is a give and take between the performer and the audience, but only up to a certain point.

When you remove playing like yourself from the search of forming your sound, you're missing all of the surprises and emotion and phrasing and specialness and character that only you can bring when you play, and that's what makes you great! You can't be great by restraining yourself. You can only be great by letting yourself free.

I remember thinking, "If I could just sound like so and so, then I'd really have it." Well, that person may have been great, but to think like that causes you to lose value in yourself, and if you don't value yourself, the audience never will. To swing, you have to trust yourself, and if you don't trust yourself, you won't be able to swing. Actually, having talent at all really comes from having the *courage to display your talent,* which is just another form of trusting yourself. Trusting yourself is key.

Finding your own sound isn't just about skill or talent really – it's about being yourself, and knowing that what you've got to offer is just as special as anyone you look up to. It may sound crazy to think that because it may seem egocentric or ridiculous, especially when you're young. But if you're going to be a musician, you have to form your sound around being yourself, and you have to see value in your own unique character. That's ultimately what sets you apart and leads you to what you seek – your own sound.

In the film *The Curious Case of Benjamin Button*, Benjamin is having a piano lesson with Mrs. Maple. She says to him, "It's not about how well you play, it's how you feel about what you play." What she meant by that is this -- if you want to have a special sound and to really play well, you have to feel good about yourself and about what you're playing. There's no substitute for how you *feel*. And if you only play well, but feel poorly, then the audience will hear a performance that was played well, but feels poor. It's as simple as that.

Dima once told me the difference between a "player" and a "true musician." She calls a "player" someone who plays well, who has technique and training, who is reliable and sounds good. Being a player is no failure, but a step beyond being a player is being a "true musician," someone who has his or her own sound, who is concerned with the whole shape and feeling of the entire ensemble, who has gone beyond the notes and the chords and is really emoting. That's what we should all go for when we play. It's not just about playing the right notes, but playing them how *you* want them to be played. You've got to go deep and feel it and you have to forget about being nervous because that will wreck the whole thing faster than a pin to a balloon.

:|| 10 ||:

Be Gone, Damned Nerves!

"Stop thinking of what could go wrong and think of what could go right."

— Anonymous

In the early years before he retired from playing professionally, my father suffered from stage freight. My mother tells me that she tried to comfort him, but things never improved. Things only became more tense and stressful once they decided to have children. Since I was too young to see this firsthand, I'm not sure what it was like for him. I think that he could have gotten over it and I still believe he could. I believe anyone can overcome stage fright. Being nervous is really just a function (or dysfunction, rather) of the ego. The ego is afraid to be humiliated or is afraid of failing or of some other possible "undesirable" result. Nervousness means your pessimism has overcome your optimism.

Think of the hypothetical failures. Maybe you don't play as well as you know you can or maybe someone in the audience isn't impressed by the performance or maybe you forget the lyrics. These things are all possibilities in performance and I've certainly gone through my share of on-stage mishaps. I've started one melody and played the bridge to a completely different one. I've dropped my bow on stage, I've totally forgotten the lyrics, I've played thousands of horrid notes, I've introduced one song and played something else, I've accidentally hit the drums, I've accidentally hit the bass, I've tripped, I've knocked things over, music has gone flying, violin or microphone malfunctions have occurred time and time again, I've said things into the microphone that nobody can recognize as English, you name it. I'm sure there will be hundreds of more mistakes! Bring them on. Let them come! I like the education. I'm not afraid to be humiliated. To be honest, I've become fairly comfortable with the feeling of nervousness. It sounds contradicting, but to me it's like creative juice. I'm not afraid of being nervous; I'm just nervous.

When you really examine these different scenarios that are playing through your mind like a movie, how much power do they really have over you? Is the core goal of the performance only to play as well as you know you can, to impress everyone in the audience, and to remember the lyrics perfectly? These are all things that you may aim for, but for me, the goal of the performance is to feel good when I play, almost exactly what Mrs. Maple said. I know that if I can feel good when I play that I'll play well. It's not about playing the fastest or most complex solo, or about flooring everyone in the audience. If they're not blown away, they're not blown away. If I forget something, I forget it.

I have learned that if I *really* want to blow the audience away and to play my best that I can only do it by focusing on how I feel when I play. And I want to feel good! I never want the audience to feel bad, so I never play with a negative emotion or a negative feeling inside me. I want the audience to be uplifted, not dragged down. If someone buys a ticket to see me, I want to thank that person by giving an uplifting performance. One thing I would not do is sing a bunch of songs about an old relationship and how bad I feel for myself and how there's no hope in life. I can't believe that some artists do that. Unbelievable.

Perhaps if I'm playing a blues, there will certainly be some level of sadness, but the point of the blues is to say, "Things are bad now, but I'm going to make it through!" If I am playing ballad and it's about heartbreak, I want it to feel heart broken, but at the same time I want to convey the richness of love despite the pain of the heartbreak. Somewhere in my sound, usually right in the center of the emotion, is a steady, deep love for what I'm playing. Now that isn't arrogance. It's gratitude. When you feel great, you can play great. You can also think of it like a great dessert. You take a bite; you taste one flavor, maybe one more, maybe one more after that. There are layers, different notes that you sense, just like perfume.

That's the question you have to answer as an artist. How do you want people to experience whatever you're giving them?

You can't play great only because of the kind of instrument you have, the equipment you buy, the venue you're playing, who's in the audience, who's on stage with you, the clothes you wear, how loud you are, the tempos, the notes, how much money you're making or any of that stuff. You can only be great when you feel great. It must come from within you.

Also, when you realize that nervousness creates more nervousness, it's important to take a deep breath and realize that you don't want to walk straight into what you're trying to avoid – ruining your performance. The only way to do that is to take calm control of your mind, to stop playing the movies in your head about what will go wrong, and then to pick up your instrument or open your mouth and to just be yourself.

George Shearing, one of my favorite jazz pianists said, "Can anybody be given creativity? No. Only equipment to develop it if it's in them in the first place." Where does creativity come from? Joy! Now I know what you're going to say. Depression and heartbreak are also vast sources of creative expression. That can be true, but one needs the energy, inner strength and the joy of actually writing the song or playing it on an instrument for it to reach the world. Too much depression leads to what we see so often in creative geniuses, early death. So I don't really believe that sadness and darkness are true creative fuel, because even if all you want to do is play the blues, you can't play the blues if you're dead. You've got to want to live, and that takes joy.

Don't suffer an early death. Early death symptoms could include having zero work ethic, constantly living in the past, seeing every situation in the most negative light possible, and also being a naysayer. Naysayers are often suffering from an early death. For a musician, symptoms may include being jealous, playing with no feeling, playing like they are scared, and never smiling at the audience. Other early death symptoms may involve hating yourself and everything that you do, always thinking that whatever you've done is not good enough and is always too late. Another similar symptom is thinking that you're not worth anything great so there's no point in trying. Other symptoms could be having poor taste in things, doing things you don't want to do with your life, exhibiting a loss of integrity or general humanity, and fighting with people over tiny and insignificant things. These are all symptoms of an early death.

To be honest I can't stand these people, the people that walk around in their dead bodies with their dead opinions and dead faces, with their egos blaming and judging everything and sucking the life and fun out of anything they touch. I refuse to suffer an early death. Joy is a great way to keep death out of your life. Don't look around and say that there's nothing to be happy about. *You* must be the thing to be happy about, or you must find something around you to be happy about. Look out into the world and see if you can count all of the wonderful things you see. *You* must bring joy to the audience's hearts and faces. That is why they pay you. *You* must have joy or you will be dead until you die.

⫴ 11 ⫵

Joy Makes You Brilliant

"Neither a lofty degree of intelligence nor imagination nor both together go to the making of genius. Love, love, love, that is the soul of genius."

— *Wolfgang Amadeus Mozart*

You've got to be happy if you want to play happy. Some of you are already thinking, "...ah, but there are so many brilliant artists that created amazing art out of deep pain and suffering." I would agree with you, and would add that I feel sorry that so many great artists suffered on such a deep level throughout their lives. However, talent is not reliant upon sadness, and as Eckhart Tolle explains it in "The Power of Now," true creativity arises from inner spaciousness and peace, not from turmoil and depression.

Once Dima and I were sitting at her dining room table in her apartment in Miami talking about what makes certain people so brilliant and in some cases, timeless. We came across many factors like determination, integrity, vision, hard work, and other qualities that great artists (and great people in many fields) have, but what we finally agreed upon was that joy is the main determining factor in brilliance.

Joy spreads like wildfire. The greatest artists in history have all inspired joy in their audiences. In everything from Classical music to blues to jazz to pop to funk to rock and other genres, you'll see that the greatest artists in these genres all were able to spread happiness in one form or another. This is true of the greatest dancers, filmmakers, poets, painters and all sorts of creative people. Some of them were very unhappy people, but at least they found happiness in their craft, in the work that they were doing. You have to find happiness *somewhere* in your life if you really can't find it everywhere. Clark Terry, one of the most delightful and well-loved jazz musicians of all time said, "Your mind is a positive asset. Use it for positive thoughts."

Fear has a hard time existing in the presence of joy, so already, if you are feeling joyous, you are filled with a desire to spread joy, to uplift the audience, to exude confidence and most importantly, to be yourself. So joy already gives you a foundation for sounding your best and for getting your message to your audience in the best possible context. Joy also fosters determination. If you want to succeed and you are optimistic about succeeding, you're much more likely to do it. You can't succeed if the perpetual background is that you feel suppressed and wronged and cheated and starved. Break out of that! Free yourself.

One time when I was about 10, I found myself in one of my mother's violin concerts called a barn dance. My mother and her violin teacher colleagues liked to put these on for all of the kids and the parents a few times a year. We would all dress up in our blue jeans and white tee shirts and bandanas, and we'd learn some of the basic fiddle repertoire and perform it altogether in the barn. There were other festivities and food afterword. People would dance and take pictures and sometimes there was a professional band that would play before or after all of us kids.

During this particular barn dance, there was a fiddler called Brian Wicklund visiting the Suzuki program for the week, and he performed with his band at the barn dance. After they played a couple of songs, I marched right up there and started playing along with the band. I didn't know any of the tunes they were playing, but I found a way to play along anyway. I went for it, totally on intuition! I was too young to care about being good enough or what anyone thought of me. I just wanted to smile and play. I fit right in even though I was about half the height of the other musicians in the band. That's the joy of performing. We don't need to go on stage fearing everything. You can just have a good time.

Everyone is looking for a way to feel free, to feel strong, to feel inner peace. Unfortunately for many people including myself at times, the ego is constantly trying to drag you down, back into your problems, back into your fears about your playing or your life or anything else. In reality, if you're able to hold on to feeling joy, you'll realize that it is actually very powerful and strong, and that it builds on itself over time. It doesn't disintegrate or slip through your fingers like sand. Every moment in your life that you choose to strengthen your inner field of peace and joy will make it grow until it is easier and easier to come back to it and to stay in it for longer and longer periods of time. This becomes especially useful in times that are stressful like when international travel plans get changed, or on stage when someone in the audience is acting like a loon.

Regarding what I was saying before about joy and freedom, if you are able to feel this way when you play, your audience will be able to feel it too, like a vast wave washing over many individual shells. In this respect, you have a lot of power, or rather potential, to transform your audience and to transform the world. If you can get on a stage and inspire joy in people, there's nothing you can't accomplish.

You don't know what you're capable of as an artist until you feel the strength and depth of your own inner joy. In that, you'll find vast amounts of inspiration, motivation, determination, hope, courage, inventiveness, integrity, excitement, creativity, patience, and many other components to being an artist that often seem lost when you're unhappy or when your inner environment is just too agitated to come up with anything brilliant in the slightest.

Why is it important to spread happiness? Unfortunately, today's world rewards sadness and insecurity. Feeling true happiness, true love, being truly intelligent, having inner beauty, or true outer beauty for that matter are qualities not seen as "cool" today. Going out dancing with a man means having sex with your clothes on in a nightclub with fake music and terrible drinks where nobody talks to one another. Being a genius today means that you made a neat drum beat with a computer program even if you've never heard of Buddy Rich or Tony Williams. "True love" isn't true unless you put it on Instagram, and I'm not sure if many 24 year-olds know how to spell or define integrity. They probably think it's a nightclub or a band at Coachella.

I think that having integrity means doing what's right even when nobody is watching you or cares what you do. It also means doing what will make the most sense in the long term when you could easily compromise that vision in the short term in exchange for money. No amount of money is a comparable prize to living a life of integrity, and no amount of money can make you feel as big as you truly are when you're doing something that makes you feel small and worthless. Money is a finite reward, and it often comes at a price much greater than the reward itself. Integrity cannot be bought or sold and sticking to it buys you infinite inner freedom, something money can never give you. That doesn't mean you can't have integrity and make money at the same time. Many people can and do. But if the question is which is worth more, the answer is always integrity. You can't know that until you choose yourself. There's a saying I read somewhere that goes like this, "If you don't take a risk, you'll always work for someone who did."

The sad reality is that there are many corporations and famous people who profit by making millions of other people feel insecure. There are entire industries that count on people's insecurities about where they eat and what they say and how they dress and what they do on Friday night and how big their bank accounts are and anything else you can think of. It is an absolute shame. It should be the opposite. Nobody should try to make someone feel lack to make a profit. We should make one another feel joyful to make a profit, and some of the time, we should do it for free.

Another problem is that people are afraid to be weird. Take Michael Jackson for example. Everyone agrees that he was great. Michael Jackson had a lot of weird characteristics and details in his musical and personal style and that's what made him *him!* People can't stand the idea of being weird so they just try to be cool and our culture suffers because of it. We idolize people with hardly any talent or vision because they do something "cool" like wearing see through clothes or miming playing the violin in a video with flames and lasers in it. I often wonder what these people would be doing if they instead 1) stuck to their integrity and 2) weren't afraid to be weird. Then they could do something more than whatever the latest fad tells them to do and they could also put all that energy into uplifting and inspiring people to stick to *their* integrity and weirdness. It spreads.

But let's get back to the negativity in art, the current fashion statement of the mundane and hopeless. I'm talking about the "don't you see how much pain I feel" people whose only other songs are "Never mind. Fuck it. Let's do cocaine," and the everlasting hit, "Rip my clothes off right now."

Let's talk about music, songwriters specifically. I'll put these three types of glum and overly relied upon songs into three basic categories. Despair, blasé and copulation. Some people say that the lyrics in these types of songs "help us not feel so alone in our sadness," or "are a much needed escape from daily life."

I don't want to help people escape from daily life by bringing them down, by making them more numb and pessimistic. I don't think that's right. We have a responsibility to inspire one another to live as much as we can. When we are able to play out of a context of joy, the audience is able to actually be uplifted. What kind of world do you want to be in? There is no need to keep spreading insecurity, desire, negativity, lack, jealousy, regret, pain, sadness or heartbreak to more and more people when you can heal them right now with joy. And is healing not brilliant?

Let's talk about inner strength, because joy comes from there too. Some people feel that inner strength comes from a religious figure or a god within. Whether or not that's imaginary, I feel inner strength coming from within *me*, right here and right now. I don't feel that I need anyone or anything else to give it to me. I feel it as I am. I'm motivated by love for myself. Love is the greatest motivation and fear is the worst. I mentioned before that when you do something out of love it's more likely to result in success and to create more success. When you do something out of fear it's more likely to go wrong and to carry with it an unintentional, undesirable consequence. Love is real motivation. Love yourself and you will motivate yourself!

Whoever loves something will likely work at it a lot and then will become a master. If you can find something that you really, really love, your motivation becomes endless. You can become a master through love. Love lights up the pathways in the brain, so I would venture to say that when you love something, you might be enabling the use of more of your brain's potential. And once you tap into that, you can do anything.

:|| 12 ||:

Perfection and the Future

"If I had my life to live over again, I would have made a
rule to read some poetry and listen to some music at least
once every week."

– Charles Darwin

O ne thing that really bothers me in art is the fad of artificial perfection. It arose so quickly that most people don't know it when
they see it unless they are professionals in the field in which it's
displayed. Or, even worse, they are professionals that have agreed that the
level of artificial perfection is acceptable and that we should just move on,
explaining that it is a sign of progress, a newer, higher standard.

Movies, music, TV, images and even food have become perfected to
such an extent that it's hard to even remember the way things used to be.
We look at computers more than we look at the outside world.

It may be true in some sense that movies and TV are more entertaining now, although I don't personally think so. Magazines think they need
to Photoshop their images to keep selling copies. There is no defense for
artificial food whatsoever, and the problem with artificial music is that
the public doesn't realize that what they're listening to is not real. It's not
human. The use of live instruments in recordings and in live "concerts"
is so rare now that young people (especially in the United States) don't
have hardly any idea whatsoever about how to dance to live music of any
sort. They don't hear human salsa bands, string quartets, jazz bands, funk

bands, rock bands or solo instrumentalists anymore. We have enough DJs. We need more high-level *live* music.

There are many art disciplines that are suffering from a strange desire to achieve this high level of artificial perfection. Artists now feel pressured to hold themselves to a ridiculous standard that even the greatest artists in history would have failed in front of. Jimi Hendrix didn't record with a click track or auto tuned vocals, Picasso's paintings were not edited after they were finished, Norma Miller's swing dancing routines were never done in dozens of takes spliced together, and supermodels in the 1950's looked immeasurably more beautiful and healthy than supermodels today.

You may not believe this, but I know of a children's hospital that actually uses Photoshop to edit the artwork by its patients on a computer because the hospital believes that the artwork that they create is not perfect enough to display without being edited by a professional to "clean it up" or make it more "striking" first! What an outrageous and ignorant thing to do. Of course when I confronted them about this they denied it all even after I saw it being done with my own two eyes.

The problem is not the production of fake-sounding, fake-looking, phony material. The problem is that the public wouldn't know the real mccoy if it hit them square in the nose! If the public were more interested in being uplifted, perhaps they'd see a symphony or dance to a nice Brazilian band on a beach. Maybe they'd go hear a real singer with real musicians or watch a ballet or an independent film, one that wasn't made with five million dollars of explosions to keep it "interesting."

There is hope! I've noticed in London that people care so much more about experiencing live music and other types of art than they do in The United States. In London, the public makes reservations to hear jazz and many shows will sell out before they even begin. They stay for the whole show, both sets, and the audiences are eager to meet the musicians afterward. They spend more time experiencing art, so they know what they like and they know how to tell the real deal from something else. I wish that more Americans could do that too.

Now I know that there are many great artists throughout history who have told us that true art must reflect the people and the opinions of the time. But I'd like to suggest that perhaps these artists didn't have the foresight to see just how far music, for example, has traveled from what it was even in the 60's, just two generations ago. If we were to truly reflect the people and the opinions of the time I don't think any of the greatest operas, ballets, symphonies, concertos, classic jazz, funk hits, disco hits, rock anthems or anything on that level would be performed anymore. Hell, nobody would write any new original music that even comes close to the greatest music of the past.

So then why do we perform this stuff? Why don't we just accept the standards of the time we're in? It is because we are trying our damndest to elevate humanity and to remind them of what they are missing. We're trying to remind them of the vast beauty and depth that exists in the world's greatest music, wherever and whenever it comes from, and to use it to enliven and inspire people. That's the task of today's musicians.

In all honesty, I'm proud to not be reflecting the people and the opinions of the time. I am proud, however, to bring people something unique, something special, something truly deserving of their attention and respect. We're playing music, right here, right now. Here is something to contemplate. The philosopher George Edward Moore said, "A great artist is always before his time or behind it."

I may have mentioned this before, but it has always pissed me off that my parents and grandmother couldn't make enough money playing in the symphony or in their trio to eventually retire. In the United States, the arts are not given the priority, the respect, or the support that they deserve by the general public, by people who hire musicians, by record labels and other companies who control and distribute music and by the government. I'm sure that this will change one day, when more and more people realize just how valuable high quality performers and artists are for culture.

Already there are thousands of programs all around the world that educate young people on the importance and the beauty of the arts, especially in schools. And, as I've seen from playing in the hospital every week, kids love art. They want to do it, they want to see it, and they want to learn it. I see how many kids are deprived from seeing and hearing great art and when they do, how dramatically it transforms them. I saw it in the parades I played with Jon Batiste in Harlem, as a kid in my mother's Suzuki program, in high school in Idyllwild, and on countless other occasions.

In many other parts of the world, indigenous art forms are such a part of the culture that the general public for the most part doesn't need an education in them. They're already experienced in every day life on the street, at restaurants, on the square, wherever the people go. Jazz is America's only original art form and one of its greatest cultural contributions to the world. Jazz should be appreciated *that much* in America, among a multitude of equally stunning art forms that all people can share.

:|| 13 ||:

Jazz is Timeless

"The bottom line of any country is: what did we contribute to the world? We contributed Louis Armstrong."

— *Tony Bennett*

Something I've been thinking about lately is what makes great art timeless. Right now in the world of jazz there is a lot of discussion going on about how far you can go away from the basics of jazz and still be able to call it jazz. In fact, there are so many debates about the word "jazz" itself, the "direction" of jazz (if it has any), and the legacy of jazz today that it would make your head spin. I don't like to get into those types of arguments because I feel that they miss the point, and the point for me is beauty. All of these details and opinions come and go and change over time. What fascinates me is that all great art is timeless in its beauty, so I'm going to focus on that.

Have you ever noticed that a great performance still moves you decades after it was recorded, or a great composition still moves you hundreds of years after it was written? That's because it exists on a very high artistic level of excellence that resonates out of the confines of culture, language, nationality, public opinion, and time.

I'll try to explain this using something hopefully we all have experienced like viewing a beautiful piece of visual art, perhaps in a museum somewhere in the world. Some of my favorites are Van Gogh, Matisse, Cézanne, Monet and Gauguin. When you look at the art as it exists today, it is current. It may be decades or hundreds of years old, but as it exists now, it is part of our current world. We don't look at a work by Picasso and say, O.K., we need to make this current, so let's add some neon colors, some flashing lights and some other stuff and then it'll *really* be great! No, we don't do that because we respect Picasso's timeless, beautiful work. He created the work from his own brilliant mind, without being guided solely by trends and fashions and of-the-moment "artistic styles" that were not made to last. He painted from his soul and when something comes from your soul you don't mess with it.

We understand, as viewers of his great works, that to tamper with them or to somehow change them in an effort to try to make them more "cool" or "exciting" or "now" would be a foolish venture. His paintings are as beautiful as they can be, simply existing *outside of time*. If you want to be timeless, you have to create on a high level, straight from your soul. There is no substitute or shortcut. Anything new or old can be timeless. It's not about when it was created, or by whom. It's about how great it is. Somebody could paint the greatest painting ever painted tomorrow. It wouldn't be easy but it could happen. It's a matter of opinion, of course, but the point is this.

I hear so many artists of different disciplines create with this sense that the past was magical and extraordinary, but now everything has changed for the worse, so there's no use "living in the past" and trying to create something old-fashioned. But when people think that way, they are limiting not only their personal taste but also their potential to create freely and without the chains of pessimism weighing them down. They're also limiting how much they'll love and enjoy their own work and I think that's a shame too.

Let's get back to appreciating art. If you're going to appreciate it, you need to have a deep understanding of that art form's eternal nature and eternal beauty. To try to change it in every little cultural moment would make it unrecognizable and remove its timeless essence. When you do that, a lot of people will ask what it is and get bored with trying to figure it out, just like what happened with jazz.

It's very simple. The fundamental basis of jazz is (1) the swing rhythm and feeling, (2) the blues form and sound, and (3) improvisation itself. Jazz music requires these three things, swing, blues and improvisation, to be represented at one time or another in the music for it to be recognizable as jazz. The eternal beauty of jazz is that it's an art that doesn't come in and out of style -- it's timeless like all great art. Tried and true. All art is timeless if it's great.

Most new art that has no footing in the past is not likely to endure. We look upon the great films, visual artists, choreographers, filmmakers, musicians, composers and fashion designers and wish that we could tap into that energy, that genius. Well, it's easy to understand what goes into creating all of these great works if you look at them carefully. You just have to understand the artist's vision and their *key ingredients*, and you can't ignore those pieces of information when you go off to do your own thing, that is unless you don't want anything to do with any of the artists you admire. That's always a choice too.

Isn't it incredible to sit down and listen to an old recording and hear how people used to play and sing? I always love hearing someone like Tony Bennett. I love listening to him connect the phrases in his own unique way or hearing him take a breath or a pause now and again, as if he were talking to you face to face. It's a shame that you don't get that kind of personal naturalness and expressive storytelling anymore. I hope that some people continue on in that tradition, of doing full, live, human takes. And doing them *well*.

Sometimes it makes me very sad that Tony is one of the last people in the world performing the American Songbook, year round, for millions of people. I hope that this music continues to reach humanity all over the globe, but we'll need some high quality singers and instrumentalists to commit to it. There are many wonderful musicians and singers who touch on this material, but very few if any who perform it in every show on the level that it requires and deserves.

Let's get back to what I was saying about full takes. There isn't just one way to make a great album, but there is definitely something truly magical about walking into a studio with nothing and walking out at the end of the day with something. It's like a great artist who sits at the paper and when he stands up, there's a drawing. Magnificent.

There's no science to it, really. You just go. Oscar Peterson said, "Some people try to get very philosophical and cerebral about what they're trying to say with jazz. You don't need any prologues, you just play." These days in any kind of music, the style of the tone has changed. The tone of voice, the tone of the instruments, the tone of just about everything has become so smooth, and I don't mean smooth like a flower petal, I mean smooth like a facelift. It's not easy to record with a band or an ensemble, or to sing a full take without making (m)any mistakes. But look – it takes practice! It's important to practice playing and singing what you want to do fully from start to finish so that in the recording and in the live show you're able to deliver a full performance rather than moments of a good performance with the majority being mediocre.

You have to start somewhere, but the more you do it, the better you'll get. You just have to focus and keep trying. Having greater technology and the ability to do a hundred takes isn't an excuse for relying on the technology. The technology should be a garnish, not the whole main course. Technology should serve to highlight talent. Talent is the foundation.

All of these different trends in recording have now caused an enormous amount of music to come out that doesn't sound or feel timeless. Nobody is "playing for keeps!" It's all meant to be thrown away. I don't want to make music that gets thrown away, just like I don't want to play for an audience that gets thrown away. We should always play like we want the music to last a long time, like we'd listen to it 80 years from now if we could. We have got to play for keeps. It means digging deep, committing to what's happening in the moment and then moving on. Think of a bird flying out of a tree into the sky, in whatever path it chooses.

I remember one violin teacher I had who was especially important to me. Her name was Maia and she was a student at University of Wisconsin, Madison, where my mother and father went to college. She contacted my mother and asked if she could teach me as part of the requirements she needed to fulfill her teaching degree, so my mother said yes. I remember how much Maia emphasized slow practice and the importance of scales and arpeggios. She also encouraged all of her students to do daily listening sessions. I think I usually chose to listen to the classical violin greats – Hilary Hahn, Itzhak Perlman, Jascha Heifetz and so on.

Maia sometimes filmed our lessons at the university because her professors liked to observe her teaching style and approach. Once when I was about ten or so I can remember playing one of the Seitz Violin Concertos along with the piano accompaniment on CD. My mom was sitting and watching the lesson, and apparently the accompaniment was much faster than my mother or Maia thought was appropriate for me at the time. But they just let me play with the CD anyway. I dove in headfirst and played the thing the best I could.

Maia told me many years later that when she showed that tape to her professors, they were surprised that I could play it at all. I'm sure it was a bit "unrestrained," but even when I was ten I didn't care that much about making mistakes or being unprepared. I just wanted to *go*. That's playing for keeps. When you play for keeps, improvised or memorized, it sounds that way. It's all about your intention and your ability to create something in the moment that will last just as it is no matter what the circumstances are. P.S. When you're an artist, the circumstances are always impossible.

It's just like when you improvise. You've got five minutes to say something in five minutes. Then the stopwatch starts and you're *in*. Improvising is not like composing because when you compose, you have a lifetime to figure out how to say something in five minutes. When you improvise you have five minutes to say something in five minutes and then you see what happens.

Each person's improvisational style has its own special flow, its own character and details that make it unique. And, even within each individual improvisation on any given song or any given take of the same song, there are special subtleties that give each one its own special moment to exist in.

Whether you're recording or performing it doesn't make a difference. It's important to learn how to use the *present moment* to achieve the highest possible outcome. We shouldn't waste it and then rely on a bunch of other people – engineers, fellow musicians, or my favorite, the ignorance of the media or the listener whose ignorance you only reinforce with low quality content -- to improve the moment that you've just wasted. To be timeless you have to practice, and you have to be able to turn on your best skills and emotions, like opening a window and watching the sunlight come right in. You have to learn to get right to the heart of the matter, right on the downbeat. The bird jumps off the branch and it is airborne. When the bow goes to the string, well there you are.

:| 14 |:

Expect the Unexpected

"So next time someone complains that you have made a mistake, tell him that may be a good thing. Because without imperfection, neither you nor I would exist."

— *Stephen Hawking*

I learned most of what I know about leading a band under some kind of pressure, whether I was in charge of the situation or not. While it's not the most comfortable way to operate, it does put you to the test. And being able to pass that kind of a test is important for a musician. I think everyone should have a few experiences like that. And if you play jazz, you'll probably have a lot of them!

One of my favorite unexpected surprises occurred just a couple of years ago, when I was playing a gig at a bar with an Irish singer and guitarist in Santa Monica. It had been raining that day, and we had just showed up for the gig when all of the power on the whole block went out. The lights went completely dark and it was getting dark outside, so there was hardly any light coming in from the street. There was a piper who came in to join us and he didn't need any power to play his pipes. But, the guitarist and I had planned to plug into our amplifiers and the guitarist was also going to sing, which he usually used a microphone to do.

Now, the restaurant was almost completely pitch black, the music and the televisions in the restaurant had shut off and everyone in the restaurant was eating quietly, using their phones and a few nearby candles for light. We were thinking about going home since the restaurant couldn't cook or serve any more food. But instead, we played a full set of totally acoustic music (which I actually prefer to amplified) as a trio in the pitch dark with just a few tables of people surrounding us. Although they couldn't see us aside from our shadows lit by a few dim candles, they were able to hear us, which provided us with this wonderful canvas of darkness and silence to play in. It was absolutely beautiful! And, if you ask me, playing this way actually improved the sound of the group.

Since we could only use the natural volumes of our instruments to project the sound, our dynamics had a greater range. We also listened more carefully to one another, so the moments of impromptu arrangement and improvisation were done with more attention to detail. I had to figure out how to get the music to reach the people in the audience when they couldn't see me, and how to communicate with the two people I was playing with when we could barely see each other. We were less distracted, more in tune, more rhythmically in sync, and I would venture to say more emotive as well. I'll never forget how much I learned in just those 45 minutes.

Another time, when I was living in Madison, I was about to perform at the local high school. I can't remember what I was going to play, but it was some short Classical solo or duet with piano. I was about 13 at the time I think. A few minutes before I was set to go on, a lady walked by me backstage and her dress caught on one of the pegs of my violin. It flew out of my hands and landed face down onto the tile floor. I still remember the sound it made. When you've heard a violin hit a hard floor a few times in your life, you never forget the sound. It gives me chills just to imagine it.

She gasped and immediately started to panic, thinking she'd broken some incredibly valuable violin and that the concert would be cancelled. I stayed calm and quickly formed a plan. My mother was at home nearby, so I called her and asked her to bring me her violin. I told her that my violin was broken, and I believe she asked me, "Is it totaled?" *Ha!* I thought that was hilarious. No, it wasn't totaled, but the bridge and the tailpiece and many of the other pieces on the top needed to be fixed, and my father took care of those later on.

At that age, I played a 3/4 size violin which is slightly smaller than the regular full size or 4/4 size violin that I play now, the size that my mother had brought me as a replacement. It was a challenge to adjust to her instrument because she used a different type of shoulder rest, and her violin was wider, longer, and much louder than mine. I only had about five minutes to adjust to her instrument, but I remember I kept my bow. I ran through my piece once back stage and walked on to play. It wasn't a flawless performance, but it was one of my best performances that year. I had committed to the moment and done my very best, and that's all you can ever do!

One time in the early 2000's when I was about 12 I was performing with a group of violinists in a resort hotel lobby in Wisconsin. During the middle of one of the pieces, one of my friends who was playing behind me threw up on my shoe. My mom was leading the show so I just stood there and kept playing, feeling the vomit slide down my foot. I'm sure I left the stage after that piece was over. That was some good training in the "On-Stage Mishaps" category.

Here's one more story that lands in the same category. I was about 21 and I had been asked to be a guest with a singer and big band somewhere in Downtown Los Angeles. I was waiting on the side of the stage to be called up when I suddenly realized that I just *had* to use the ladies room immediately. While I was sitting on the toilet, I suddenly heard, "...and now welcoming to the stage, the incredible Nora Francesca Germain!" My eyes almost popped out of my head. I missed my entrance but luckily they let me go on one song later.

There was another time in the late nineties when my mother had picked me up from the park on the way to play a concert. She had brought some black and white clothes for me to change into at the venue. I went into the bathroom to change just before the concert and in my clothes from the park was a hornet that stung me right in the arm as I was changing. It was quite painful and itchy but I had to go on and play the concert anyway. Ladies and Gentlemen, watch out for the tiny flying hazards!

As I mentioned before, some of the most rewarding work I've ever done is volunteering at Children's Hospital Los Angeles under the Mark Taper and Johnny Mercer Artist Program. I've held a weekly post as the only solo musician volunteer for the past three years. I really enjoy playing there for the kids and their families and friends. Over the years I've played for thousands of people and gotten to meet so many wonderful, spirited children. I take requests when I'm there, something that most other musicians don't often do, especially on the violin. I find it both challenging and creatively energizing!

With so many generations and cultures of people represented there and often all in the same waiting room, I have to be ready for anything. They could ask for Beethoven or jazz music or Taylor Swift or Star Wars or Harry Potter or Selena Gomez or Stevie Wonder or a song from a Disney movie or a Broadway musical or a hit from the Beatles or Aerosmith. Then, even if I haven't ever played the song requested before, I have to come up with a solo violin version of it that the people will recognize and enjoy. It can get interesting. I never run out of things to play!

The first few times I played at the hospital I didn't take requests but now, as long as the patients and families are in the mood for it, I think that a requests-based musical format is more entertaining and personal for them. Sometimes they dance or sing along, and if I'm playing for parents who are waiting for their kids somewhere, they sometimes take videos of me that their kids can watch later in their rooms or wherever they are. That way they can feel like I'm really playing a song for *them*. It makes it a lot more personal.

I can't tell you much else about the unexpected due to laws that protect patients, but nothing will surprise you more than seeing sick children getting up and dancing when you play. It's amazing to see these kids inspiring one another and their parents to remember the joy in life. The kids exude pure, uninhibited joy, something most grown ups are afraid to show. The kids are not self-conscious. They are living reminders of what it is to live in the present moment.

In 2014 I was crossing a street in West Hollywood around dinnertime during a nighttime rainstorm and was hit by a Jeep. I was carrying my violin on my back and a few other bags in my hands. I was in the cross walk with the walk signal but the driver didn't see me. I ended up landing several feet in front of the car on my bottom in the wet street, still with my violin on my back and all of my bags in my hands. I started shaking and crying immediately and I was alone. I didn't know what to do, so I called a friend who picked me up and drove me to an urgent care clinic so I could be examined and x-rayed. You wouldn't believe this, but when I opened my case at the clinic (that's the first thing I did), my violin was in tune! Also, having the case on my back may have saved my life because without it, I could have broken my back or worse. Many people don't survive accidents like that, so I know how lucky I am.

Recovery was slow and unpredictable even though I didn't break any bones. In my head I kept feeling the wetness of the car hitting me whenever I crossed a street, even in plain daylight. At times I felt that the trauma I was feeling wasn't all that *real* since other people didn't experience it or see firsthand what had happened to me. When you get into an accident alone, you recover alone. You're in pain alone and you go to physical therapy alone. It took months for me to feel more or less normal.

Luckily, along with the pain of recovery I also had gratitude. I wasn't just grateful for my existence, but grateful that I got to continue experiencing life. I appreciated everyone around me, I appreciated playing the violin, I appreciated the kind of life that I have, the time that I have to do with it what I want, the freedom that I've been given to use that time the way I choose, and for just plain not dying.

During this period of gratitude I stopped by Hotel Café to hear Zane Carney play a solo show as he often used to. Suddenly I was overcome with this feeling. It was a deep, very alive, very awake sense of gratitude. The curtains were more red, the people looked more friendly. The music was more sacred. The moment seemed more of a privilege. I wondered to myself, "Is this true reality?"

I started to well up watching Zane play. We were in a room full of young people who were all there to enjoy and support his talent. There we all were, together, experiencing life in this one room. What a gift! When you experience a moment like that, a moment that could have been your last, every day for a long time after that feels like an extra gift that you could have very easily never seen. It's a gift whether or not you can see and feel it. The gift is just waiting for you to take it in.

:|| 15 ||:

Gimme a High Five and Keep Jammin'!

"I've just got to maintain my passion for what I do."
— Leonardo DiCaprio

There are many times throughout my life that I've wanted to give up on music. Most of them were temporary, maybe lasting a few minutes or an hour or so. In my early days at Idyllwild, there were times when I felt ready to quit playing forever. Now, I know that the feeling of wanting to give up is just a silly trick that my ego plays on me and I know better than to entertain any such thoughts. I know that it's not truly what I want, that quitting won't bring me any satisfaction, and that there really is no reason to quit. I'm not going to quit because I know I won't.

You know you won't quit if you have long-term grit. If you're determined not just on certain days or certain months but over the long term, then you won't give up. You have to play the shit gigs for no one. You have to go through these types of experiences. When you go through them and you continue to go through them with dignity, you won't find any solid reasons to quit.

I know what you're thinking. "I can think of a million reasons to quit right now!" Well, I'm going to go through a few of them with you here and explain why you shouldn't give in to them. Give someone a high five and keep jammin'! First, I have a story.

When I lived in New York I felt a deep loneliness for most of those two years. I experienced moments of inspiration when I got to play with Jon like I had wanted to, or when Dima and I went to see someone fantastic

97

play at The Blue Note or another club. Other than those times, I felt more or less that I didn't have a purpose of my own. I had gone through all of that work in Idyllwild only to come to The New School where I felt that I'd all but failed. My potential added up to nothing. It was just my boots full of rain every day and lectures on dissonance. And more rain, and more dissonance. What was it all for? This was not the future I'd dreamt of and worked so hard to create.

There were some people at the school that inspired me and gave me great advice – Cecil Bridgewater was very kind, and I was also taking lessons for a brief time with the great jazz violinist John Blake Jr. who reminded me of Marshall in some ways. John was gentle, encouraging, deep, honest, a great listener, always thinking about music, always prioritizing his students. These were all qualities that Marshall taught me were the most important qualities for a teacher to have.

One day, John came in for our lesson, sat at the piano and told me he was very sad because his friend Dr. Billy Taylor had just died. I told him I was so sorry and I wished there was something I could do. He told me that because he was so sad, he wanted to play a blues with me and cry a little bit so that's what we did. He just sat there at the piano and we played a blues.

After that, he told me some stories about Billy and about their friendship. I can't believe that John even came to the lesson when he was feeling like that. John was an amazing man. He was honorable, kind, sweet, and strong. I'll admit I didn't get to know him very well, but he was a great teacher to me even if it was just for a short while. He passed away in 2014, but I'll always remember how much I cherished and respected him. He taught me a lot about life, just by being around him. In this New York cacophony I had finally found someone who could really uplift me.

John taught me to never quit in the long term because he never quit in the short term. Even in his grieving, a time of deep sadness and personal loss, he found the energy and enthusiasm to come and give me a lesson. I'll never forget that. I think John approached life one day at a time. If you can show up today, you can show up for your whole life. It's kind of like sports. You win the season by winning each game. You win each game by completing each play.

So what are the reasons many of us want to quit from time to time? I know I had mine. Perhaps you want to quit because the amount of time it will take you to actually reach your goal or your dream is very long, and it will be a difficult, time-consuming venture involving humiliation and evolution and failure and all of the things that go into making something great. Well, you should never quit something because of how long or hard the road to get there is. You need something called determination, and it's not easy to keep up. But, what it can give you is perspective to keep moving forward, even if you're in the middle of a particularly treacherous stretch of the road. Plus, when you're working, time flies! If you don't think you can make it, resort back to determination. It's those of us who don't quit who find success more than any other single factor. Don't be luke-warm. Don't become depressed and discouraged. You have to keep the fire inside your heart and your mind and your hands burning.

After my time as a formal student of Marshall's ended, that was the last of the best jazz education I ever had. And, truthfully, besides that semester I spent with John Blake Jr., I taught myself most of what makes me sound like me on my own. I picked up a lot of things on the fly and I questioned my own taste and style. I've only been working on it for about eight years so far, but I know I will be working on it forever. It takes a long time! You just put in the work and try to get better. Itzhak Perlman, one of my favorite violinists of all time said, "I am playing the violin, that's all I know, nothing else, no education, no nothing. You just practice every day." Marshall tells me these days at his beautiful age of 76 that he is just now beginning to feel like he can really play. And Ellen DeGeneres said on her show recently that her success came after 25 years of hard work. Not 10,000 hours or 10 years or whatever. *25 years!!!* So don't give up now.

You may find you want to give up if you feel that you're not good enough. Well, it may be the case that you're not good enough to get it right away, but it's not the case that you can't get it ever. You have to hang in there. Building up your skills and your talents is a valuable thing to do. There have been many things in my life that I couldn't get right on the first try, but the more I worked on them the more I learned about them. If you're unusually talented and you can do something perfectly on the first try, then you haven't really learned much from the experience. If you have to keep at it for a longer time than you had originally expected, or a longer time than most people put in, then you will learn far more about life, about staying focused and about believing in yourself.

Never shy away from putting in more work in order to keep up with your dreams. Put in the work, even if it takes decades. Not to mention, when you finally get to where you want to be, wherever that place on your journey is, imagine how great you'll feel.

Perhaps you're losing hope because you've been comparing yourself to other people too often or too seriously. It's great to look to other people for inspiration. But to seriously form your opinion of your progress and to maintain your self-esteem by comparing yourself to others at every turn is to rob yourself of all of the things that make you *you!* I used to compare myself to classical violinists thinking that I was nothing next to them, but would forget about all of the things that I could do that made me special.

Everyone, *everyone*, has something special and unique to offer. It's not just about talent. It's about being yourself. As a side note, sometimes I think about how wonderful it would be to perform some of the great classical violin repertoire, and perhaps someday I will! But when I think about it, the best way I can describe my feeling about doing it is that it would be a bit like Fred Astaire dancing in Swan Lake. Maybe he could have done it very well, but we wouldn't have seen the most extraordinary facets of him.

Everyone that ever did anything got an idea from someone else. We all share inspirations and there is no doubt creative lineage in every art form. However, that's no reason to compare yourself all day every day to someone else. No two people have the same life, the same experiences or the same strengths. It's all about being yourself and remembering that what you have and who you are is special, even if you can't see it in this moment. Don't think, "Oh, that person is such a star and I'm such a loser." Well, with that attitude you will be. You don't know how much someone will love and appreciate your talent in the future. You may not even know how much someone appreciates you right now! There are so many great artists that felt that what they created wasn't all that valuable, even at the height of their fame. Vincent van Gogh only sold one painting while he was living and was poor his whole life. Now his body of work is worth billions.

I'm not trying to say that if you're a genius you'll only make any real money after you're dead, or if you're truly great, nobody will appreciate you while you're living. The point I'm trying to make is that just because you don't see how great you are doesn't mean you're not. Plus, everyone that became great was once a young kid with a big vision, so don't worry about where you've come from or if your family is rich or poor or any of that. You can accomplish anything you want to exactly the way you want to do it as long as you don't give up. Don't allow anybody to tell you anything about you. What and who you are is for you to decide.

Maybe you want to quit because you feel you're on a plateau of mediocrity and things aren't moving ahead as quickly as you had wanted them to. Maybe you're young, maybe you're old, but you're searching for meaning, for worth, for money, for someone to care. Well, I care! So if you have been looking around for someone to care about what you're doing, that takes care of that!

I'd be willing to bet that there are a lot of people in your life that care about you too, but perhaps your perspective has been obscured. Let me refresh you. This might be a little much, but try to get on this level with me here for a moment. The universe has been forming for 14 billion years or so, and the Earth is over 4 billion years old. Some way or another life formed, and life has been evolving for billions of years now, too. So here you are on this glorious planet Earth complete with plants and seashells and friends and family, and to top it all off – music! Your mind and your soul are evolved and brilliant enough to play a song.

Maybe you play in a bar once a week for tips, or maybe you're touring the world with a rock star. Maybe you're a music teacher, helping to enrich and inspire the lives of young people. Whatever you're doing, you have the opportunity to see value in what you're doing in the *big picture.* You have no idea the effect that your singing or playing has on other people. No idea! And, you've got to know, there are millions, maybe billions of people living on the same tiny planet as you and I *right now* who will never, ever be able to press down the smooth white key of a piano or hear the sound of an audience's applause, big or small.

So remember that if you're playing anything at all that it is a privilege, an honor, and a brilliant stroke of something like luck that has made it all possible for us to know one another and perform together. We are able to share our songs, share other people's songs, and share songs from all over the world, songs from hundreds of years ago, or the song of the moment. All of it is a miracle of unspeakable magnitude. Treat it as such, and remember that what you've got is special.

When you feel that you've reached a plateau and everything's the same, that can sometimes be a fantastic sign that you're ready for evolution, or that change is around the corner. When you feel that you've had enough of what you're doing, take it as a beautiful reminder that we never stop growing, never stop learning, and never stop creating! Don't get down on yourself for feeling that you're on a plateau. Everyone needs to be on a plateau at least for a moment to get to the next level. Some plateaus last years. That's just how it goes sometimes.

Sometimes I feel that when I practice I'm not getting any better and I keep doing the same things over and over and it's all for nothing. Then, usually very soon after that, I'll have a breakthrough or something great will happen. Hard work pays off and sometimes you need to hang in there a little longer to see *how* it's going to pay off.

You may want to quit because you are feeling misunderstood. If we simply let go of this desire to be understood by other people, we can avoid a lot of negativity just in that one decision. Unfortunately, until you're able to let it go, there are a lot of reasons that being misunderstood can give you a feeling of worthlessness. Sometimes the people around you, even your family, can become jealous of you, envious of your young age, your perseverance, your intelligence, or even your positive energy. Other times, people make you feel small because they want to control some aspect of your personality or future. Maybe they feel threatened by you.

Still one more possibility is that they simply don't "believe" in you or are unable to realize how possible your vision really is, that is, if you ever bothered to tell them about it. When people don't believe you it's usually because of narrow-mindedness or ignorance about what it is you're trying to accomplish. I don't think people shoot down each other's ideas on purpose. People do that because of doubt and fear. Or maybe they simply don't realize how good you really are. They just don't realize what and whom they have in front of them.

Just like a person at a garage sale sells a valuable antique for a dollar, they'll make you feel like your dreams are garbage. *They just don't know what they have.* Only you and a few people very close to you will understand what you are and how great you can be. Keep those people close and keep your mind sharp. Your surroundings, your bank account, and what people think about you aren't always the best indication of your worthiness or potential.

There may be times later in the future that you need to remind yourself of this. And remember, if your dreams scare you or seem impossible, that's a good sign that you should run after them with everything you've got!

Some people become derailed by discouragement, especially if it comes from a person or place that is perceived to be a source of truth like a record label executive or a famous person or someone close to your heart like your mom or dad. You may feel crushed by some "advice" that someone gives you. Well, it's very important to examine how much this person's opinion *really* matters to you at the present moment. You have to ask if this person or group of people is qualified to judge your talent and vision.

Don't assume that someone who has power or money or fame knows what is possible for you or even has a clue about how to *interpret your vision.* That includes your family. I have been extremely fortunate to know several people in my life that understood my vision and respected it right away. These people became my mentors and closest friends. Not everyone understood me, and not everyone will understand you. In these moments, you must be strong, not only in the presence of your imagined possible future success, but right here and now, just as you are.

Sometimes it can take time for you to see what your purpose is, and once you've found it, you may find another! One time my brother said to me, "Nora! Your music is the return of jazz as a popular music. 7th graders in Alabama need to hear your music. Old men in China need to hear your music. The ladies of the night in Amsterdam need to hear your music." That made me laugh, but it also made me *think!*

How can we use the music to bring them all together? How can we get them all dancing, clapping, singing and enjoying the music as one? And how are we going to introduce jazz to people who don't already know about it? Where and how are people going to hear it for the first time? Suddenly there was a fire, a purpose to what I was doing.

Finally, some people feel like quitting because what they are trying to do seems impossible. Maybe there exists some sort of a technical challenge, maybe society doesn't believe in your idea the way you think it could and should, or maybe there is too much ignorance about it. Well first thing's first. You can't revitalize something if you're tying that something to the very circumstances that point to the need for its revitalization. For example, don't say to yourself that you want to save the symphony even though nobody wants to hear symphonies anyway. Think rather about how you can share and spread *your* love of the symphony. Come at it from optimism.

Many things seem impossible until they are actually accomplished. If you are truly working on something that in your lifetime you can't see coming to pass, then maybe you will be a vital link in the research or progress towards whatever your idea may be. Think of how many scientists made unbelievable breakthroughs but never lived to see where they led. Who knows what the distant future will be like? Nobody. But your passion and enthusiasm may be able to make it a better place!

If you're dealing with a technical challenge, you have to keep trying, at least that's what the scientists say. If you're playing an instrument, maybe you need to put in seven hours a day for a few months. Who knows. You won't get there procrastinating. That's for sure.

One more thing. The present moment is always unique. The conditions that you are experiencing now whether they are between you and someone else or they involve where you are living or an opportunity you have been presented with are not guaranteed to repeat themselves in the future. Don't let a moment pass you by. The opportunity, these conditions, may never come up again. It may seem that things will go on the way they have been. You'll have more chances; there will be more time. They'll still offer me the same deal tomorrow. He'll still love me next week. I can always visit next year. Well, believe me. If you see an opportunity don't waste it. You could wake up the next day and realize that what you wanted is now gone forever and there's nothing you can do about it. Take it while you still can.

:‖ 16 ‖:

A Few Thoughts on the Now

"What day is it?"
"It's today," squeaked Piglet.
"My favorite day," said Pooh.

– A.A. Milne (Winnie The Pooh)

I recently read the book, "The Power of Now" by Eckhart Tolle. I think it's one of the most important and illuminating books of our time. One thing the book mentions that is especially useful for a young artist (or an artist of any age) is to not seek peace or satisfaction in the future. If you constantly live your life seeing your future works, achievements, earnings, awards, tours, or whatever you're doing as your chance to feel good about yourself, then you will always and forever miss the only chance to actually be happy, which is now. Why can't you feel happy in those moments of achievement? You likely will, but only for a short time. Your ego will look to something else for you to crave in the future. We shouldn't just feel fulfilled one minute or five minutes out of every year. We should feel fulfilled for a good portion of every day, right here in the present moment. I'll never forget when Scott Cowie asked me, "Nora, you ever wonder why some of our friends who are more successful than us are not as happy as we are?"

He understood the point. Seeking yourself, your "full" self, your "finished" self or your "new and improved" self in the future is to lose the self that you have right here and now. The self that you have here and now is the only one you'll ever have! You can't "have" anything in the future, for as the future comes, it's experienced as the now. Artists are constantly pouring our time and focus into future projects, and this is a wonderful thing to do with life. We aim to share our talents and beauty with the world. Fantastic! However, to do this while constantly feeling that your current state, your current set of skills, your current surroundings and your current achievements are not good enough is actually a bit insane.

All of the things that really matter in life, the things that cannot be taken away, are things that exist within you already. They're not really "things" at all. Your character, your spirit, your motivation, your work ethic, your love for yourself, your talent – these things truly last forever and don't exist only in the moments in which you get an award or exit the stage at a sold out concert. If you're in the middle of working on a new project, don't feel worthless until it comes out. Your project won't last forever. You don't need any experience or any physical object to give you worth. The outcome is not your worth. You being able to reach the outcome is the worth.

The outcome is great, but what lies within is greater. What lies within *is all of the characteristics* that allow the outcome to be realized. This is the reason that we all must feel complete now. In this moment, we have all of the things that last forever, the things that truly matter, the things that exist outside of space and time. This is where your *true* accomplishments lie, not in a glass case for everyone to see. The way I see it is this; be grateful for what you have now while working towards what you want in the future.

You already are who you want to become. This is another valuable lesson from Eckhart Tolle. As soon as you realize that, you are able to create much more expansively and freely. Don't resist it by saying, "But no! I'm not who I want to become yet! I still have another album to release! I'm not finished yet!" You never want to start a project hanging on the finished product like it's a rope around your neck. If life were all about the finished product, then the thousands of hours that Matisse spent painting wouldn't be his life. His "life" would exist in his paintings. This is not so. His beautiful paintings exist for us to enjoy today, but his life was in the words he spoke, the time he spent doing whatever he did with his days when he wasn't painting, in the hours mixing paint, in the hours his brush glided over the paper, in the days and hours and seconds of life. Breathing in and out. Drinking water. Eating a grape. Every second. *That* is life. Some old piece of canvas is not life, however glorious the painting on it may be.

Whatever you do with your life, make sure it's honorable enough and worthy enough that it'll stand up in front of the people you respect most in the world, including yourself. Always be reaching higher. Don't take less than you deserve and don't *be* less than you deserve. Everything you want to be is already within you, but you must be true to yourself and act on your inner truth.

Be in the now. Look around. Take a deep breath. The only way to practice being in the now is to practice being in the now right now. All you need to do to be free from the past is to decide to be free from it. Fear is not real. It's an illusion. There is no fear. There is no past and no future. The totality of you exists here and now only. Thank you, Eckhart, for your insight and guidance. It is indeed transforming the world.

:| 17 |:

Be Your Own Best Friend

"Let everything happen to you. Beauty and terror. Just keep going. No feeling is final."

— Rainer Maria Rilke

I can remember many times in my life when I had to face a difficulty on my own because there wasn't anyone around to help me. Sometimes the difficulty was internal and sometimes it was something in the outside world. Part of growing up, I think, is learning how to look after yourself and how to be your own best friend. Sometimes, you're all that you've got. But the good part is that you, on your own, are much stronger than you think!

My parents taught me a lot about being my own best friend when I was a kid. That experience has taught me that nobody can take the wind out of your sails. They're your damn sails. Being your own best friend comes with a lot of responsibilities. One of them is reminding yourself that you're not alone just because you're alone in this moment. Another one is looking out for yourself when you're about to go down the wrong path or you're about to make a poor decision. Being your own best friend also means knowing when to say no to someone or something and that saying no is a necessary and healthy part of life. Being your own best friend is also about taking care of yourself emotionally, physically and all other ways too. It involves encouraging yourself when you are feeling down, and telling yourself, "I can do this." Even when your patience and optimism are worn paper thin, you have to dig deep and give yourself the kind of advice and love that you would give to your best friend.

Appreciate your life, your health, and your time on the Earth, and be gentle on your body. It's the only one you've got. Realize the beauty of life on a deep level and be there for yourself when you're in trouble or not well. Focus on your health and on living a long time! Don't do anything that hurts you or makes you feel bad. Just walk away. The consequences of not being your own best friend can be catastrophic. For example, since starting school at USC in 2011, two of my friends passed away, both under 40. Actually, one wasn't even 30 yet. They were both absolute genius musicians. They were well loved and admired all over the world.

One was an immensely talented piano savant and I got to know him a little bit when we were studying jazz at The New School before he moved back to California. The other was one of the greatest saxophonists in the world and I had the pleasure of playing with him several times in Los Angeles. We used to talk about all things life and music until the wee hours of the morning. I have fond memories of both of them.

It's such a waste when these things happen, and they happen too often all over the world. It's a waste of talent, a waste of friendship, a waste of love, and a waste of life. I wish that these two could have been their own best friends when they needed it most. Maybe it could have made a difference.

I read somewhere that the best relationships and friendships are between two people that want to be together, not two people that need to be together. Love must be greater than desperation. In life we experience tragedy, death, illness, conflict, and many difficulties. If you can be your own best friend, you'll realize that you don't *need* anyone. You may love certain people very much your whole life and be willing to do almost anything for them. That's beautiful, but if you can be your own best friend, then you can survive anything on your own. And, the love that you give to people will not depend on them giving it back to you. You will give it freely and it will be freeing for people to receive it, not burdensome or conditional.

There are times in life that require a lot of deep, steady, inner strength that aren't tragedies too, like going on stage for the first time or telling someone, "I love you." You may need some inner strength to accomplish an *inner* goal, like deciding to embark on a new project or improving your health. In these moments, being your own best friend will get you through. Never, ever underestimate the power of your own inner strength, especially when motivated by love.

:|| 18 ||:

Be Strong

"The truth is, being a healthy woman isn't about getting on a scale or measuring your waistline – and we can't afford to think that way. Instead, we need to start focusing on what matters – on how we feel, and how we feel about ourselves."

– Michelle Obama

There are a lot of women that have inspired me, who epitomize what I was just talking about – inner strength. We can learn to have inner strength by seeking the example of others. To be honest, it hasn't been easy for me to find a great mentor. There aren't many female musicians. There are lots of singers, but it's not easy to find women who play instruments primarily, and it's even more rare to find one who leads her own band. Then when you want to find one in jazz you'll really be searching for a while. I certainly have been, but I've learned a lot just by observing and researching women, even ones in completely different careers than mine.

For one reason or another, here are some women whose lives and accomplishments have inspired me; Lillian Hardin, Louis Armstrong's wife, who died *while playing the piano on stage* at a memorial concert for Louis, Shirley Horn, who Marshall credits as his greatest teacher and mentor, performers like Nik West, Norma Miller, Esperanza Spalding, Susana Baca, Carole King, Andrea Motis, Sheila E., Adele, Alison Balsom, Nicola Benedetti, Anne Akiko Meyers, Nina Simone, Camilla Wicks, Janelle Monáe, Cecile

McLorin Salvant, Dee Dee Bridgewater, Lady Gaga, Beyoncé Knowles, Taylor Swift, Nadja Salerno-Sonnenberg, Ella Fitzgerald and Cassandra Wilson. I also find Michelle Obama, Jane O'Meara Sanders, Princess Diana and Jane Goodall to be great sources of inspiration.

In addition there are many others who are friends of mine and inspire me in my daily life like musicians Alison Burns, Carol Chaikin, Genevieve Artadi, Patrice Rushen, Sherry Williams, Dima Dimitrova and Michelle Tseng; Deborah Brockus, a wonderful dance instructor and choreographer who I studied with at Idyllwild Arts Academy, and Richelle Gribble, one of my best friends as well as one of the most creative visual artists and thinkers I know. I'd also like to thank all of the women in science, athletics, medicine, environmentalism, foreign aid, the military, women at NASA, in the government, the entertainment industry and in other fields who continue to accomplish truly extraordinary things. You might also notice that throughout this book there are quotes by even more tremendous women who I haven't mentioned here. Bill Nye said, "50% of the people are women, so 50% of the scientists ought to be women."

First off, every woman needs some well-tailored, well-made clothing for important occasions. Women need to embrace elegance and sophistication as well as the concept of natural beauty. There are too many trends and styles coming in and out of fashion all the time, and most of them aren't worth following. Most women who follow the never-ending stream of trends in magazines have very low self-esteem and are trying to prove something that they believe is lacking internally. The answer to that is to look within, not to just change your outfit. Don't worry about being as thin as a rail or as tan as a supermodel. Brush your hair, smile, and keep your chin up. There is hardly anything more beautiful than that. I like fast cars and strong drinks and high heels too, but there are other types of beauty that go beyond these material things. They'll take you much further in life, too.

Another important thing is to be well spoken. Annunciate when you're speaking. Eliminate incorrect grammar from your speech and writing unless you really mean to use it. When someone asks you a question, respond as accurately as possible, and never shy away from a great conversation that truly interests you. It's great practice and is something that every woman needs to know how to do. Fran Lebowitz said in an interview, "We have this idea that if someone is beautiful they have to be stupid. Everyone believes that." While it may be true that many people think this way, it's also a reason for women all over the world to strengthen and act on their intelligence, rather than to accept this reality and to move on. This is especially important in parts of the world that don't support women's rights, health, independence or education.

Don't be afraid to share your ideas about something. Never keep them to yourself because you're afraid that people around you aren't intelligent or open enough to understand them. They may not be, but don't wilt in front of them like a weak flower just so you can fit in. Don't be afraid of being indelicate.

On the other hand, be careful about who you share your ideas with. Sharing a big idea with a small-minded person can result in a very painful and uncomfortable conversation, and it may cause you to second-guess yourself for no reason. No need to waste time proving yourself to someone who wouldn't recognize greatness if it kicked him or her square in the ass. You'll never argue your way into getting someone to respect you because there is no point in trying to get anybody to do or believe anything. They'll only believe it or do it if they are internally ready to receive it, if they already know it to be true and you are in essence *reminding* them. You never know when people will be ready to hear a new message or understand a new idea. They will when they're ready, or they just won't ever be ready. There's nothing you can do to make somebody ready to hear you. All you can do is tell the people who *are* ready. Work with *those* people.

Don't let the wrong man hang around you for too long. Don't let him control you, put you down, make you feel small, waste your time, or influence who you are in a negative way. If he's the wrong one, he's the wrong one. You have to free yourself so that you can go on and do all of the things you're going to do, man or no man by your side. A brilliant woman in the hands of the wrong man is an absolute shame. Romance is not the most important thing in life. If you're a woman, remember that you can do anything on your own. You don't need a man to give you permission or support. I believe that if the right man comes along that you'll know it. You shouldn't have to convince yourself he's the right one. You've got other more important things to do. This has always been my view on the matter of men.

Don't be afraid to challenge people's ideas and to question what they say. Some people may say that this creates unnecessary conflict, and of course you don't want to start an argument. But if someone says something that you feel should be clarified or may not be true, don't be afraid to say it. It's a sign that you're paying attention and that you're not to be fooled with.

Don't be afraid to be the expert in something, and once you are, don't be afraid to be recognized as the expert. If you're the expert, that's what you are. Don't apologize for being the best. Don't say you're the best *female* such and such. If you're on the top, be on the top, and don't apologize for being a woman when you got there. It's true that there are some roles in society that are perceived to be more naturally feminine than others, but that can all end with you right here and right now if you want it to. Be passionate about what you're doing. Make the most of the opportunities in front of you.

Don't be discouraged by men (or women) who are not used to seeing strong women in action. They might tell you that you're cold or too serious or too intense. If you mention that women are treated and paid unfairly (which they are, all over the world), they may roll their eyes and call you a feminist. Well what the hell is wrong with that? It's good to be a little bit shocking. You may find yourself in social situations dominated by mostly men and having to introduce yourself because nobody will bother asking you your name. They may assume you're someone's girlfriend who's totally uninterested in the discussion, not realizing that you're actually an expert, and that you could be mentoring them tomorrow. So don't be afraid to tell them who you are.

Be straightforward. Don't say things in a more attractive, polite, soft way than you normally would if you don't want to. Don't apologize for things that you're not sorry for. Don't say you're sorry when you mean to say thank you. Don't act like you're intruding or imposing if you're not. If you want to ask somebody if they're free on Tuesday at 2 o'clock, then ask them if they're free on Tuesday at 2 o'clock. It's a simple yes or no question. You don't need to be liked more than men just because you're a woman. What you need is to be respected and taken seriously, so don't forget to put on your ass kicking shoes when you leave the house, even if your ass kicking shoes are just a pair of sneakers.

Take care of yourself. Mind your health and your family. Be honest with what is going on around you and look it straight in the eye. Prioritize your wellbeing and your longevity. Never take your health for granted and never neglect yourself on any level. Don't slip into a vice or into a bad habit to cope with something, because these habits can ruin your life and ruin the lives of people around you. Be a strong woman. Breathe, try to solve the problem, get some help if you can, and move on. Don't be weak. It's always easier to solve a problem than to perpetuate it. It may look the opposite way, but in reality, dragging your feet always makes you heavier.

Remember that you've got to be on board with yourself. This goes for men too. Don't look for support from people around you when you need to make a positive change. It's likely that you already have their support but fear is making it hard to see that reality. Oftentimes the vote that you think you're missing is your own vote. Remember to always be a friend to yourself, not an enemy to yourself. Having support from people around you can make whatever change you're undergoing a smoother one, but you can't do anything if you're not onboard with yourself.

Finally, don't be afraid of change. Change is constant in this universe. If you're the exception to societal rule, don't be afraid. If you're about to change the way something works, don't be afraid. If you're changing the way people see women in your field, don't be afraid. To hell with what people say about you now. Just think about what they'll say after you succeed.

:∥ 19 ∥:

The Art of the Audience

"To have great poets, there must be great audiences too."
— *Walt Whitman*

I n 2015 I went back to Idyllwild to play in one of Marshall's Black History Month celebration concerts. He puts one of these on at Idyllwild Arts Academy every year in February. I graduated in 2009, and although I had been back numerous times since then, this one in particular felt special to me for some reason.

In essence, it was a variety show. Marshall's vision was to incorporate dance, poetry, drumming, singers, several configurations of jazz ensembles plus The 14 Strings, which is Bob Boss, Marshall Hawkins and me, into one show. Performers of all ages, cultures, and styles all came together to create one big celebration, and the current jazz students from Marshall's program played too.

Usually in this type of scenario, most of the material is performed totally impromptu and unrehearsed when you walk on stage. This kind of thing used to scare me but now I am much more used to performing in this way. Even when I have no idea what's going to happen and it's totally silent on stage, I've learned to just stay calm and alert. Don't panic and don't make any sudden movements.

In the years I studied with Marshall, he would often give us the opportunity to make something up, sometimes the ending piece to a concert, sometimes the opener. Whatever Marshall saw in his head we tried to pull off. It was always out of thin air and total silence. Marshall would just cue you to *do something*. It makes having a melody in mind or a tune to go on almost a luxury! But even when there *is* a chosen piece of music, a ballad for example, the task is then to make it special. How can I make it one of a kind? How can I make the audience remember this forever? You don't just want to play it, get it over with and walk off. You want to really do something extraordinary, but you can't do anything close to extraordinary if the audience isn't there with you.

I noticed that night that each performer was given total silence by the audience. This is something very potent, because it gives the performer the ability to do things that a mildly quiet room doesn't, like having extreme dynamics, taking your time building up an arrangement or an introduction, having the piece begin from and return to total silence, or in my case, showcase the violin as a focal point in the musical expression of a ballad. You can't do that with a mildly quiet audience, but when they are silent, you can.

Not only did they provide silence, but also they provided many of the performers with standing ovations during the show. They screamed, they clapped, they stood up and danced, they yelled, they laughed, they hollered when they liked what the musicians were doing in their solos. They were totally present, allowing the musicians to get inside their souls and make them feel something. It was really powerful. The whole show was a lesson in *audience* performance.

There's more an audience can do then just give attention and context to a performance. They also gave new confidence to the students that played with us, confidence that enabled them to take more risks, to go to the extremes, to emote more dramatically. It enabled them to be better performers. The same thing that happened to me when I was a student! It's amazing to feel an overwhelming amount of love and support from an audience when you didn't expect it or even think you deserved it. It can really change the way you play. When the audience is great, they are telling you that they believe in you. They trust that you will dazzle them and they are giving you the respect and the space to do it.

In high school I can remember walking into a private lesson with Marshall and just sitting down and crying for most of the lesson. I told him everything about my parents, and he explained to me that there is an invisible line in front of the stage. He told me that when we perform, the audience has an emotional and spiritual choice to make. They can either cross the line and be alongside you, alongside the performers in the spirit of love and creativity, or they can simply watch the show. He explained, in his own way of course, that the stage is like a sacred place where there are both no friends and no enemies, because the music is greater than these distinctions. He also said that if I chose to keep performing, the stage would protect me from all of that bullshit because music is more powerful than that. So long as I kept playing, whatever bullshit was on the other side of that line couldn't even touch me. It was like music could save me from anything and anyone. The stage was a pure place, a haven from conflict, and a place that only music could have the last word. And beyond that invisible line, *anyone* could have the last word. I knew where I wanted to be. I wanted to be on stage, on the stage side of that invisible line. It hit me *real* hard.

I'm thankful for the patience, attention and support from all of the people that came to see me play in my early years at Idyllwild. *They* are a major reason that I was able to feel free enough and fearless enough to try things. In those years every performance was an experiment in itself. It's where I learned to play. I was learning live. The audience can lift you up! They can be part of your education.

A lot of young audiences these days aren't used to leaving much space in a show because most musical acts in pop, R&B and dance music play shows with virtually no silence in them. In fact, the way a lot of the world's most popular artists perform, there's no time *to breathe* because your whole performance is synced up with a backing track or a metronome of some sort. Imagine how terrible "Bohemian Rhapsody" by Queen would be without the drama and inflection that made it so iconic.

When you're playing a show that's on a timer, there's no time to deviate, no time to improvise, no time to take an extra solo if you're feeling especially magical. On the opposite end of the spectrum, some people think that watching a show that begins and ends in silence is too intense, like trying to keep your eyes open for a long time without blinking.

I really enjoy sitting and listening for a while, relaxing in my chair, taking a deep breath, and experiencing a performance. A great symphony or ballet will come in and out of silence many times in an evening. All the best concerts do, even ones at Madison Square Garden. They leave you on the edge. There is surprise. There is drama. There is *human interaction.* There is room for improvisation, room for audience participation, room for error, and best of all, room for the real deal to help the audience to remember why it's the real deal.

It's strange that we feel the need to occupy ourselves every second of every minute with audio or visual stimuli. When there's no space, the art can't be fully enjoyed. It's like eating a gourmet meal as fast as you can. You can't really enjoy it that way. So the next time you go to see a concert, try to give the performer your full attention. Look at that person. Stop talking. Turn your phone off. Wait for something to happen. Get the most out of that ticket. Take it in.

:|| 20 ||:
Choose Your Mentors Wisely

"Children must be taught how to think, not what to think."

— Margaret Mead

Find mentors that love you and want you to succeed. Go to the people who make it clear to you that they want to be in your life, they want to help you on your way, and they believe in you. It's all about how you feel when you're around them. You have to really ask yourself how someone makes you feel. Trust your gut.

If you play violin, a mentor doesn't have to be someone who also plays the violin. You can have mentors in many different categories. I certainly do. It's great to find mentors who can guide you toward your aspirations, but there may be more than one type of person who can help you get there.

Choose mentors who respect your freedom and want you to figure things out for yourself, who aren't too eager to start driving the car for you. It's important to find someone who can give you clear and honest advice, but doesn't make you feel like a fool for wanting to think for yourself. In fact, a great mentor will trust in *your thinking,* and will even strengthen your trust in yourself when it's the right time.

Not all popular mentors are good mentors. You have to find someone who is right for you, and that may not always be the most popular or famous or wealthy person. Be careful not to follow in someone else's footsteps so closely that they totally obscure your own. Don't become a mini version of someone else. Don't let your mentor impose what he or she would have liked to do on you. A mentor is supposed to help you make decisions and create success in *your* life, not in his or her past life.

Think about your mentor's character. Try to see how much integrity and moral fiber that person has. See what motivates this person and makes him or her feel fulfilled. Try to understand this person's creative principles and methods for communicating. Think about how much you trust this person.

The best relationships of this kind come out of trust, and you can't trust anyone who doesn't listen to you. Marshall, the greatest mentor I ever had, listened to me. He listened to me by watching me, by giving me opportunities, by never passing judgment on me, and by giving me love. He listened to me by letting me go off on my own. He listened to me by answering my questions in an open-ended way so that I could interpret them myself. He listened to me by giving me unconditional love, unconditional trust and unconditional patience, no matter what happened. He let me figure out a lot of things on my own. He knew I had to live through them and experience them to know what to do and how to proceed.

When something went wrong he would assure me, not blame me. When I was angry with someone he taught me to let it go instead of taking my side. When I made a mistake, even if it made him look bad, he would show me what I had learned instead of asking me why I did it. He was the kind of man who would choose an ugly but delicious homemade cake in tin foil over one on three tiers made by a gourmet chef. *That's* the kind of mentor you want.

Listening and hearing are *not* the same thing. Just because someone can hear you doesn't mean that they're listening. You have to keep an eye out and keep your bullshit meter on high alert. Like I said, just because someone is famous or wealthy doesn't mean that he or she is the right mentor for you. Famous and wealthy people can bullshit too. It can be surprising or even shocking to witness it, so much so that you may think of a whole list of excuses to defend your mentor with when he or she is bullshitting you. You may even blame yourself. Just because you're the one being mentored doesn't mean that you are wrong about everything and your mentor is right. Part of having a mentor is knowing when you're the one who's right and not taking less than you deserve. Don't let someone use you. You may be thinking that you need that person, but that person may be the one who needs *you*!

Whether you're old or young, you may realize that taking a good hard look at your mentors, whoever they are, may uncover some wonderful qualities about yourself that you couldn't appreciate before. When we idolize other people we tend to forget a lot of the greatness that already exists within us. Once you stop idolizing that person so much, you may discover that there are things that you do better than your mentor, or you may find something that you can do that your mentor can't. That's a good sign. That means that you're digging deep and growing on your own. It means that you're on your way to someday becoming a great mentor to someone else.

:|| 21 ||:
Send the Elevator Back Down

"You cannot do a kindness too soon, for you never know how soon it will be too late."

– Ralph Waldo Emerson

I n college, Dima and I used to write letters and emails to our heroes in music. They were performers or teachers who we wanted to meet and someday have professional relationships with. We meant well, but we didn't quite know what we were doing. It would all start out very nicely. "Dear so and so… thank you for taking the time to read my letter…"

By the end of it, we'd written twenty lines of the most over-eager, over-zealous, brown nosing correspondence you'd ever seen. Dima even used fancy stationary and brightly colored pens for some of her letters. I had written things like, "It would be an honor if you would be willing to consider the thought of meeting me on an occasion convenient to you and your greatness…"

I remember one note in particular that I sent to someone who is mentioned in this book. I went on and on about how much I admired this person and his music and then got into talking about some of my personal friends who were also musicians. Out of the blue, I wrote, "Do you know Bob?" Well of course this person didn't know my friend Bob! How humiliating.

Dima's letters weren't much better. She used phrases like, "your un-matched level of artistry" and "I would be so humbled and graciously thankful." It was really quite funny. You'd think we would have exercised better judgment than to actually send these but we just sent them anyway. We didn't usually receive a reply, but every once in a while we did!

I don't recommend going about it in the same way that we did, but you should always try to meet your heroes. It can be months or years before you actually get the chance, but it's always so worth it to wait. I've been very fortunate to get to know and even work with some of my heroes, and I know for a fact that in some cases, it was my initial letter, however embarrassing, that got the ball rolling.

Many of these people have given me a lot to be thankful for. They offered to meet me back stage or at a sound check, invited me up on stage to play, asked me to come to the studio or to have a jam session, shared a story with me, introduced me to their families and friends, invited me to stay at their houses, emailed and called with messages of encouragement, supported my music, and gave me back stage passes or a spot on the guest list. I hope that I can be that person to another young musician some day.

Clark Terry, one of the greatest trumpet players to ever live said that helping young people to succeed was the premier focus of his life, even more important to him than playing. I think that I may ultimately share this dream. Music gets passed down from generation to generation. When you're in touch with young people, when you're encouraging them and giving them a moment with you to learn something, you're not only providing them with a beautiful experience, but you're also motivating the next generation as a whole to carry out the beauty and the spirit of the music! What could be more worthwhile than that?

Unfortunately, I feel that many older musicians don't share the same passion and enthusiasm for inspiring young people that Clark did. All I know is that I want to be like that someday. I want to have young people playing alongside me. These kinds of experiences enrich everyone, including the audience. At the very least, inviting young people to be around you before or after the show provides them with a warm greeting and exciting experience. Many older musicians don't know how much that's worth, or maybe they've forgotten.

Sometimes older, more famous artists aren't willing to speak out about younger ones, even when the younger ones deserve it. I don't see what the older artists are afraid of. If I see someone who is great, I'll say it loud and proud. It helps people to go places. It helps them on their way. Why wouldn't you help someone? Maybe it's because they're afraid that if they did something nice for one person that they would be required to do something nice for someone or anyone else. That idea is just the fear of obligation or of doing the wrong thing, and fear is never a good motivating force.

I've seen some older artists treat younger artists like fans even though they perform together. It's a shame that it takes so much effort for young people to break through (i.e. hit it big), even in the eyes of their own colleagues and mentors. Young people have their work cut out for them in terms of putting out music, going on tour, engaging the public, making money and navigating the music industry. Having respect and support from older musicians shouldn't be part of that hard work. If you can play, you can play. That's that.

It's important that we all share our respect for one another. There isn't a pecking order in music the same way there is in a hospital or in the military. In music you can move up anytime and anywhere, no matter how experienced or famous you are. It's just like what Marshall said. On stage there are no friends or enemies. The only master is the music.

You can consider this a call to action for all of the touring artists, bands, producers, engineers, concertmasters, and virtuosos and anybody that receives messages from young people. I hope that if you receive an eager phone call or a message from a young person that you respond, if you can, and go meet him or her in person. You never know the kind of effect that your words or your meeting may have on both of you. It could change your lives. Even if it doesn't, just remember how much this young person respects you and what it was like for you when you first met one of your heroes.

Everybody that ever made it had at least one hero or mentor that agreed to spend some time with him or her early on, so it's time to pay it forward for whoever did that for you. And, even if you're not meeting the next genius in whatever it is you do, that young person may go on and repurpose your kindness and generosity for some other beautiful task or calling.

I hope that everybody reading this who has a career with fruits worth sharing is listening to me when I say this: Share the limelight, send the elevator back down, and give some young people a chance to get to know you. It could be one of the greatest things you ever do.

If someone ever calls me up or messages me with that kind of enthusiasm, I will be sure to reply as soon as I can! If I can't reply with a way to meet, then at least I will try to offer a few words of encouragement. Even with a gift that small, the potential for healing and inspiration is limitless, and as karma reminds us, it always comes back around.

:| 22 |:

The Beauty and Character of Jazz

"Life is a lot like jazz. It's best when you improvise."
— George Gershwin

One of the things I love so much about jazz is that anybody can play it, anytime. Jazz is about the spirit of the now. You have to be light on your feet, ready for anything. Jazz is a lot like nature that way. Nobody knows what's going to happen in the next moment or in the one after that, or next season or next year. Nature has great capacity to improvise. Take for example the way vines grow on and around the surface of a house. No two vines are exactly alike and there are no straight lines. Chemically and genetically they may be the same, but their shape and direction can never be duplicated.

In jazz even if you try, you can never play something the exact same way twice. I was just thinking about jazz music recently, about the balance between right and wrong, organization and chaos, beauty and conflict. What I came up with is that jazz sounds like shit if you don't play any wrong notes. But it also sounds like shit if you don't play any right notes.

Wynton Marsalis explained that when you take a solo, what you're really saying is, "I am." I even wrote a blues once called, "Blues I Am." That's another beautiful thing about jazz. Everyone is free to leave his or her own personal mark on the music; from the way you play the melody to the way you play your solo. Your mark could be a cadenza in the beginning or the ending, or perhaps your mark is the feeling of the rhythms and how you play them in such a way. Maybe your mark is the quality of your tone. Your mark could be anything.

In jazz you are free to make that statement on your own. You don't need anyone's permission and you don't need to copy anyone else. I like that the best jazz musicians celebrate their own uniqueness, their own marks. They don't try to be the same as one another. They share the differences in their sounds. Every great jazz musician has a sound. You can identify each musician instantly by his or her sound. In jazz your task is to create a unique sound, a unique way of playing. Your uniqueness may be very subtly different from someone else's uniqueness, but regardless, the difference is there. It's in the details, just like nature.

When it's done right, jazz music also has a way of keeping the audience on the edge of their seats. There can be moments of silence, leaving the audience hanging on the next word or note. There can be feats of technical mastery. There are melodies that can be played so perfectly and so deeply that they bring a tear to your eye and transport you to another place in your heart. In jazz there are so many ways to surprise and dazzle the audience. It's limitless. There are no rules about playing too fast or too slow, to quiet or too loud. The only rule is to express yourself to the music's highest potential.

Another thing about jazz is that anyone, young or old can play it. People from different parts of the world that don't speak the same languages are all able to play this music together, because the language of swing doesn't need words. It's a higher level of communication that doesn't require words or symbols. You just play. That always astonishes me.

Jazz also has a way of healing people. It can make them feel free or make them want to dance. It can remind people of something beautiful that they had forgotten about. It's music with a wide range of possibility. There are just enough rules to keep it together, and just few enough that you can take the audience anywhere you want to go. You can change the key, sing in a different language, change the time signature, or the tempo. You can play heavy or play light. You can sing a song in a whisper and the next night loud as all hell. It heals people to see this kind of contrast and creativity. It's human interaction, audience participation, and the balance between extremes. Some of my favorites are Jon Batiste, Clark Terry, Antonio Carlos Jobim, Nancy Wilson, and Frank Sinatra.

Another beautiful thing about jazz, as Sonny Rollins said, is that jazz can absorb so many other types of music and still be jazz. You can add almost anything you want to it like a melody from the radio, from an opera, from a musical, from a folk tune, a nursery rhyme, a traditional song from any country near or far. You can even make a tune swing even if it wasn't meant to swing in the first place! I always demonstrate this with, "Twinkle, Twinkle, Little Star," which was one of the first songs I ever learned to play. You can "jazzify" just about anything as long as the feeling is within you, and when it is within you, sharing it with people is one of the most glorious feelings in life. Someone asked me recently, "How do you teach classical musicians to swing?" I said, "Put on some jazz music and tell them to start dancing."

:| 23 |:

Jazz and Classical

"I have discovered three things which know no geographical borders – classical music, American jazz, and applause as the sign of the public's favor."

– Jascha Heifetz

I've never understood why the world of jazz music and the world of classical music are so separated. I think that these two styles of music are actually a lot more alike than most people realize, but the more the performers and audiences are separated, the harder this is to see. First off, each could take a page from the other's book. I think that classical music could get rid of some of its perfectionism and the insurmountable pressures it puts on its players in auditions and performances. Jazz could become a little bit more elegant and there could be more focus on tone quality and stage presence, but that's just my opinion.

I also think it's a shame that oftentimes, jazz musicians are not really very interested in what goes on in the classical world and vice-versa. They don't know very much about how the others live, what they're thinking about, what they're performing, what their aspirations are and so on. I've been asked several times by classical violinists if I practice this "jazz music" at all or if I just go and do it. Sometimes that has really offended me. Of course I practice! I practice exercises, technique, scales, learn new repertoire, and work on all of the things that classical violinists work on, only they're focused to help me improve playing jazz instead of playing a concerto for example. The greatest jazz musicians practice just as much as the greatest classical musicians. That's for sure.

Nobody has illustrated how closely related these two styles are better than one of Disney's "Silly Symphony" short films called "Music Land" from 1935. Another one I love, unrelated to this point, is from the same "Silly Symphony" series, and it is called "Symphony Hour." It is an absolute riot. Anyway, "Music Land" is about a war between the two lands of jazz music and classical music. Each side uses its own musical strengths as the weapons, big band swing on one side of the river and the powerful symphony on the other.

As they continue to wage war on one another, a cello and a saxophone that are very much in love become caught in the middle and these two try to survive while asking their parents to call off the war. I won't tell you the ending, but I think it's fascinating that in 1935 Disney was inspired to illustrate this so beautifully. Imagine the music that was in the air at the time! Imagine the musicians who knew each other and went to see each other play! It must have been magnificent.

Unfortunately, the same type of mutual admiration and high-level collaboration doesn't occur as often anymore. Nobody performs as often anymore and the audiences for these genres have become more and more separated. Jazz and classical have both become a lot more modern, so there is less and less material that they have in common. Classical musicians don't play Gershwin and Cole Porter very much anymore, and jazz musicians don't play Tchaikovsky or Chopin. Many composers and performers have become increasingly concerned with what is in fashion in music and what the critics will enjoy. Both of these genres suffer when their musicians don't feel free to play what they like and when they don't play with one another. I'm trying to change this, which is why I love to play pieces like "The Swan" by Saint-Saëns or "Humoresque" by Dvorak. I recorded a piece on one of my albums called "Violin is Now," which was inspired by what I think a violinist may have sounded like in the stride piano era, in the 1920's. The style of stride piano is one of the most divine things on this Earth, and in my opinion, is just about the best damn use one could have for a piano. Ragtime is another. I also wrote a "Prelude for Jazz Violin," but I haven't recorded it – yet.

Unfortunately, classical musicians and instructors don't always see being a jazz musician as an asset to playing an instrument. Aside from their ignorance about the tremendous foundation of musical and technical knowledge that a well-studied jazz musician has, many of the people that make these kinds of assumptions end up being wrong and know it. What surprises me the most is that a lot of them are American. Jazz is America's heritage! Americans should know and love jazz music because it's part of our history, and it's the greatest artistic and cultural contribution we ever made to the world. All music teachers in America should have knowledge of jazz *and* other music from around the world.

The vast majority of music history's greatest instructors and educators are of the classical school. Most people can't name as many outstanding and renowned jazz instructors and educators, even though most of them were also renowned performers, just like in classical music. Many classical musicians have no idea who Clark Terry, Charlie Haden, Ron Carter or Martin Taylor are. These people upheld America's musical heritage for the next generation, just like classical violinists Ivan Galamian and Dorothy DeLay did for theirs.

The contributions these remarkable people made and continue to make in jazz are seldom known by the public because there isn't any old money in jazz like there is in classical music. It's an absolute tragedy. "You go over there and do your thing in the spotlight. I'll be over here just saving *America's* musical heritage. You're welcome."

I was fortunate to be trained by one of the greatest music educators and jazz musicians in this country, Marshall Hawkins. I know that many of his students have gone on to teach with the enthusiasm and passion that he gave to us. He passed it down *thoroughly*. Marshall didn't just teach us to be individuals. His lessons weren't some nonsense hatchet job that gave us freedom at the expense of quality. He had a fierce ear and eye for detail. He instilled in us the importance of intonation, dynamics, timing and phrasing. It was all in there. He emphasized stage presence, communication and confidence. Backstage before a performance, we would all yell as loud as we could, "KAKAWHAM!!!" That way the audience knew we were coming.

While I'm on the subject of genres, I'd like to touch on how unimportant they are. Everyone should be aware of at least some music in every "genre," like being aware of many different types of cuisine. Every culture has a flavor and some cultures have many flavors. The more you experience, the better taste you have.

However, genres only serve to distinguish styles, to highlight the subtle differences between one and another. Genres shouldn't be walls between villages. They should be signposts above them that say, "Hello and welcome! We're makin' guacamole! Tomorrow, who knows!" I don't mean to say that "genre" is a meaningless way of categorizing music, but I don't think that it's necessary. Genres are much more exclusionary than inclusive and I think it gets in the way of creativity and people's openness to following their inspirations. Artists are very quick to judge themselves, and the public just as quick to judge them. Genres serve as one more label, one more judgment, one more added piece of language that can never really encompass the true essence of the music itself. So why try describing it? You just have to go experience it and then see what you think. Record labels need to learn this, also. It's not all about the genre, people. Music is one big quilt with squares from all over the world, and some of them overlap. That's life!

The direction of an artist doesn't come from choosing a genre. It comes from the artist being him or herself first. If you go from there, the genre will fall into place. Etta James said, "I wanna show that gospel, country, blues, rhythm and blues, jazz, and rock 'n' roll are all just really one thing. Those are the American music and that is the American culture." She saw those styles as the American quilt of music. She didn't list those things and then go make an album. She played the music she loved, and that's what it turned out to be. Etta James wasn't a gospel/ country/ blues, rhythm and blues, jazz and rock 'n' roll singer. She was Etta James.

One more thing I don't understand is the reason to aim for a certain "demographic." We are all people, and old or young, we have more in common with one another than we think. Life's timelessness lies in experiences like great art, great food, in love, in nature, in travel, in humor and in community. The greatest gifts that life can offer are all gifts that we can appreciate no matter how old or young we are.

A lot of the music today is created to please certain age groups, and I think that's a problem, because as Tony Bennett explained in his wonderful film, *The Zen of Bennett*, the record labels focused on demographics and now they're all bankrupt. Focusing on a certain demographic is like taking a train apart while it's on the tracks and seeing how far each car will go. I think it's a mark of a great musician to be able to play something that everyone can enjoy. Older music and newer music can be appreciated side by side. But, if someone is making music and the idea is that nobody over 25 will listen to it because by that time they are too well informed, then maybe the problem is the music. The actor John Cleese said about comedy, "When the target audience is American teenage kids, you can have problems. My generation prized really fine acting and writing. Sometimes you have to go back to the basic principles which underpin great visual comedy."

Experiencing music, particularly music that involves international collaboration, bringing different cultures, generations, languages, styles, dances and people together not only inspires us to create and to embrace one another as an artistic people, but it also promotes peace. It shares appreciation for the astounding beauty that humanity has yielded on planet Earth, so far the only place in any universe where we have found music at all. We must continue to collaborate and to do so with other cultures and generations, for these kinds of bonds show us the profound beauty of the human race, which exists in all of us. When we are able to see that we are all connected in this way, hatred, blame and prejudice simply cease to exist. It's impossible to have these thoughts amidst a creative and artistic global community, so this is something we must all continue to build together.

:| 24 |:

You're Not Alone

"There's not a word yet, for old friends who have just met."
— *Jim Henson*

There is something very important I'd like to say. I can't even get to the rest of the chapter until I say this. Most people who know me know that I don't really like small talk very much. I like to have real conversations with people. I like to get into the deep stuff – philosophy, people's big ideas, recent scientific discoveries, and the occasional heated topic. I like to ask people what's going on in their lives and what they'd like to be doing. I ask them about their goals and their dreams, and usually they tell me.

I can't tell you how common it is that people tell me that they're disappointed in themselves. They say in one way or another, "I've had so much opportunity and what have I done with it? I don't deserve any of it," or, "I have so much talent and I just sit around. I'm so stupid! I waste it all," or, "I had so much potential. If I could just focus myself then things would improve. I hate being this way," or, "I don't have the job I want. I'm not married yet. I don't have the money I had hoped for. I'm not getting any younger and I am such a loser."

There are many variations, but I've heard people young and old, accomplished and less accomplished, rich and poor, formally educated and less formally educated all say these types of things about themselves. People are literally listening all day and night to a voice in their own heads give them reason after reason after reason for them to hate themselves, to be depressed, to blame themselves, to feel guilty, and most of all, feel hopeless at the fault of their own failure or laziness. How can you accomplish anything under those conditions? How can you even pour your cereal?

What's even more amazing is that most people that feel this way don't realize how common it is. The majority of us have been there at one time or another. I certainly have. So instead of digging yourself into a deeper and deeper hole by spending time reflecting on this guilt, resentment, doubt, fear, anger and frustration for yourself and for your life, why not make a change? Why not decide to stop wasting time and to treat yourself better? It makes no sense to walk around thinking, "I know for a fact that I've messed up my life more than anyone else in this world. I can feel it. I know it's true! Look at the facts!" It's not true and it's a waste of time, so you might as well just stop doing it. Turn that faucet of negativity off. You'll feel *much* better.

We all have to learn to 1. Stop judging ourselves. 2. Learn how to make new habits, change our behavior and make positive resolutions. If we're all walking around thinking these horrible things about ourselves all day, it's no wonder we treat one another like crap. Many of us walk into a room in fear that nobody will like us. Well then guess what happens? Many of us wake up in the morning assuming the day will be a self-designed failure – *again*. Well then guess what happens? Many of us set goals in our own minds but then the next minute think of a huge list of reasons why they'll never work and even if they were to, we wouldn't be the ones to do them. Well, guess what happens?

Our attitude is everything. We see what we choose to see. Of course, there are things we see that don't appear simply because we choose to see them, like the sun. You can't avoid the sun. I'm not talking about that. I'm talking about your *outlook*. I'm talking about the way you interpret the world around you, and the way you interpret your life and yourself. What's the frame of the picture? Charlie Chaplin said, "You'll never find a rainbow if you're looking down."

Every job, every dream, and every life has challenges. Nobody is free from illness or being late or spilling things or heartbreak or any of those things. I'm not saying that if your frame is optimistic that you will never run into problems. What I'm saying is that your frame will change your outlook when you run into problems, and hopefully, when they're not your fault, you won't blame yourself for them. If you can learn to accept when these small disturbances arise in life, you can certainly learn to accept when you're met with a creative challenge or a problem to solve. You won't see it as a sign to throw the whole thing out. You'll solve it and move on.

I don't believe that the universe "materializes" what we think. The universe doesn't care what we think or what we "pray" for. I do believe, however, that a positive attitude and positive thought *inspires positive action*, and that definitely changes the world around you. You can pray all day for your dreams to come true but if you don't get to work you can forget about it. We must hold positive thoughts in our heads to inspire us to act. Then we see change. Then we transform.

It's not easy, but we must fight negativity with optimism and true, steady, unwavering belief in success. If we do that, then our thoughts can change our lives. If we believed that we could do only half of what we are actually capable of, the world would be a very different place. Write down your goals! Plan them out! Post them on your bathroom mirror or above your dresser. Believe in them and get to work, one little step at a time.

Don't get down on yourself. That only makes it all worse. Don't get down on yourself for being down on yourself! Then you'll have layers and layers of this negativity built up. If you're unhappy because you judge yourself too often then you need to stop being so hard on yourself. If you're unhappy because you're not satisfied with the actions you've taken in your life then you need to do something about them and start making changes, even if they're small or gradual ones. Sometimes a ship changes course. Is the whole trip a failure? No!

I am too hard on myself sometimes. Learning to love ourselves and to be kind to ourselves is so important, especially when we let perfectionism and the desire for the end result get the best of us. I'm hard on myself because for most of my life, I've done almost everything on my own. All my traveling, all my performances, all my albums, all my education, all my time spent practicing and meeting people and writing music and so on and so forth has been done without a label or management or boyfriend or band or family to help me through. So because of this, I feel that I have 100% of the responsibility to make this thing work. I want a certain end result. I want it to be perfect. I work really hard so that I can see that it was all worth something.

Nobody can be focused and productive 100% of the time, but even while I know this, when I need a break or I haven't completed every single task I've set for myself for the day, sometimes I feel lazy or sloppy. I question how much dedication and determination I have, and that leads to me questioning if I've truly earned or will earn anything in my life. But in reality, I'm just judging myself much too harshly. I may be a workaholic, and I don't think that that's such a bad thing, but even workaholics need to give themselves a break and a little credit sometimes. It can feel like you're barely making any progress when in reality, there could be a lot to celebrate already! We need to see the good in ourselves, to realize that we are capable and hard working and deserving of our own approval and patience. We can't always feel that we don't do enough. We must give ourselves credit where credit is due and rest when rest is due.

Question whether or not you would judge a close friend as hard as you judge yourself. Question whether or not a close friend would judge you as hard as you are judging yourself! The answer to both of these is probably no. John Mayer tweeted something beautiful once. He said, "I wish everyone's impressions of themselves could be as good as the best impression someone has of them."

Many people judge themselves *because* they're unhappy and then they pretend not to be or cover up the dilemma with some sort of vice or distraction. The real solution is exactly what I said before. Trying one or both of these will dramatically help. 1. Don't judge yourself. 2. Make changes, right now. You'll feel so much better when you try one of those two things, or ideally, both of them. We must believe that we can achieve what we want to achieve. It's up to you to believe it. Nobody can make you believe anything. It has to come from you. You have to have the guts to get behind yourself.

Never, *ever* think that you're alone in your mind's ability to create new and interesting ways to convince you that you're a piece of crap. The key is to know that you're not a piece of crap. That's not the truth. Don't see what your ego is trying to make you see as fact. It's not fact. Your ego is just twisting your life's events so that they fit into an ugly frame (perception) and making you see it as one big crappy picture. It's an unfortunate and painful effect of the ego, but you can just as easily and quickly let it go as it arises. If you sense a negative thought about yourself or someone else, just let it go. Imagine that it floats away like steam in the air.

You can also imagine your mind is a stone and negativity is like dust or sand building up, grain by grain, particle by particle. All you need to do is turn on the faucet of *positive* thoughts and wash the stone and it will be clean. Anytime something negative tries to coat it, rinse it again. Now, I can continue to the rest of the chapter.

In life, you're guaranteed to experience feeling alone. I have certainly felt this way. There have been many times in which the people I had counted on most had let me down and I couldn't understand why. We have all been there, wondering how things could get so messed up in our families or friendships or anyplace else. Sometimes people are so caught up in their own fussing and fighting nonsense that they miss the big picture. The most important thing in life is being together and enjoying the present moment. There is nothing more precious than being around the people that you love, telling them that you love them and enjoying life together.

If you've ever been let down, then you'll know that the very feeling of betrayal is a terrible burden. This is another thing that Eckhart Tolle has spoken about. It's best to just free yourself from that burden, the burden of being a person who has "been betrayed," and to restate the story in your mind so that the betrayal is taken out of it. As many spiritual teachers have pointed out, forgiveness is not something that you do for someone else. It's something you do for yourself so that you can be freed from that burden. That has helped me a lot.

There's no time in life for fighting. There are people growing up, marriage proposals happening, recitals going on, trips to go on, bags to pack, birthdays to celebrate, drinks to clink, and you'll miss it all with the person or people you love if you're too busy fighting. There's also no time to be cold or petty or selfish. It's always better to have people around than to not have people around. And it's always better to help someone than to leave him or her in the cold. If you're able to help someone who needs it, there's no excuse not to.

When there aren't people around and you are feeling alone, remember that there is certainly somebody who would love to hear from you. There is somebody who is probably thinking about you right now, maybe half way across the world. There is someone who is wishing that you'd call on the phone or come for a visit. You've got to remember that there are those people that won't slam the door in your face, who are there for you even when you feel that there is no one you can trust and nowhere to turn.

If you just gather the courage to ask for a little bit of help, you'll realize that there is somebody who is there for you. You're not alone, because you've got a lucky star right by your side who cares about you and wants to help you. It may not be the person you were thinking of or hoping for at the time, but knowing that someone is there for you can make all the difference. Plus, you never know how close you'll become with someone who you've just recently met. Some of my best friends were only acquaintances for a while before a deeper friendship emerged. I just had to wait for it to happen.

Sometimes the people who ended up becoming my closest friends were total surprises to me. I didn't always see it coming or even welcome their friendship in the beginning. I can remember plenty of times when I met someone, thought he or she was a nice person, and then realized later on that he or she was a total genius or had a personality that really inspired me but I overlooked. You never know *who* you are meeting! You may be shaking hands with your next best friend or perhaps a future hero of yours. You may be shaking hands with a current hero of yours who you just didn't recognize! That's definitely happened to me. After learning this lesson over and over again, I try my best now to imagine that everyone I'm meeting is a genius of some sort who I will totally fall in love with. You never know how much you're going to love and admire the next person you meet, so treat everyone you meet with that in mind! At the very least, you'll be greeting people with respect, openness and compassion, and that in itself is worth spreading.

There is nothing I wouldn't do for my friends. They know who they are. I've flown across the world to be with them. They could call anytime of night or show up any day unannounced and put the suitcase right on my living room floor. I owe them my whole life and there isn't any time I wouldn't be delighted to help any one of them with a problem, no matter what it was. These people are the people that cherish and respect me, who push me to do great things when I'm afraid to do them, who reassure me that they are by my side, who make me remember who I am, who are on my side when things go wrong and who always inspire me and make me smile.

You need to have high quality, motivating friends like that in your life, people who you really admire. Sometimes they come right out of the blue. They may not be the people you've known the longest or the ones you have the most in common with. They may not be the closest to your age. I have friends who are 10, 33, 52, and 78! You never know where or when a good friend will show up, but when you've got one, take a minute to realize how precious and beautiful having a good friend can be. When great friends come into your life, don't ever let them go, and make sure to tell them how much you cherish and love them.

If you're still looking for someone like that in your life, then I'll be that person for you. You can write to me anytime and I'll do my best to respond as soon as I can. When you feel that you have nobody to turn to and you're having a small problem, or maybe a big one, remember that there is always someone who wants to help you. Just try your best, be your best, and know that there is someone who is willing to help you and who believes in you. I believe in you!

In all honesty, that's the reason why I play. I just want people to feel free from whatever makes them feel like they're alone. I want to fill everyone with courage and freedom. I want everyone to feel that feeling when you're outside in the back yard having a party and eating a strawberry and all the people you love are right there with you. I hope that when I play that somebody feels that way. You're not alone because I'm right there with you, playing for you!

:| 25 |:

Play the Horn!

"I want to do it because I want to do it. Women must try to do things as men have tried. When they fail, their failure must be but a challenge to others."

— *Amelia Earhart*

When I first set out to write this book, I didn't tell very many people about it because the people I did tell cautioned me about not coming off too proud of myself. I don't think it's my problem if someone else is too insecure to embrace the kind-hearted courage and enthusiasm of any young person. Why are certain people so quick to judge others for doing unusual or extraordinary things? And why must they point to fear and judgment first and foremost?

I think it's because there are people who feel insecure next to younger, optimistic and hard-working people. There is nothing more threatening to an insecure person than a young person with balls and talent. Because of that insecurity, they feel small and vulnerable, even when the younger people don't do or say anything directly threatening to anyone whatsoever. So, to cope with this feeling, to keep the ego intact, some people offer the younger or more ambitious ones advice. The advice is usually some form of criticism or warning, usually an attack on the young person's taste or idealism. They do this more to young women than young men I think.

Why do they do this? I don't think I'll ever understand trying to put someone in their place because they need to be taught a hard lesson. Young people have it hard enough. Everybody treats you like you're stupid and have no idea what you're doing. Everyone's saying no to you all of the time and trying to take credit for what you're doing. People use you to try to make themselves look good, and they take advantage of you and think you don't notice. Young people don't need to be lectured unless it's out of pure love. And for the people who think I'm too young to write a book, good for you. I don't think you're never too young or too old to do anything. Look at Joey Alexander, the prodigy jazz pianist. He released an album when he was 11. Should anyone tell him that he is arrogant if he wants to make a jazz album at 11? Hell no!

Something else occurred to me recently. Child prodigies are celebrated and respected a lot more than young people in their late teens or early twenties. Once you become a teenager and start going out into the world, people stop encouraging you and start discouraging you. They start to question your ambition and style. They question anything and everything about you when if you were 12, they'd give you nothing but praise. Sure, when you're 12 things are great. You don't have to take care of yourself and you're not really out in the real world yet. But then you get older and you have to figure out how to do things on your own. You have to break through, become an adult, and find your way in the business. You have to find your tribe of people, and you have to make bigger decisions. And *that's* when people start to criticize you? There are some things I will never understand.

That brings me to my next point, which relates to the title of the chapter. When I look back on all of the great legends in music, I realize how young a lot of them were when they became legends. Some of them were just teenagers when they began recording what would become their most iconic material. They may be old or dead now, but in their time, they were my age and oftentimes younger. Jazz is a young person's game. Music in general has always been a young person's game. There is no age minimum or maximum for genius.

So this is my point. Don't wait to play music or to write a book or to dance or to do anything. You're never too young and you're never too old. Nobody should ever criticize an idea just because it's too brave or too bold. If you've got something to say then say it. If you want to make something that you think can help people then make it. Whoever is criticizing someone with bravery just feels threatened or fearful because he or she doesn't have it. Well I've got news for that person doing the criticizing. You *do* have bravery, you just have to dig deep and find it within yourself. Stop knocking people down and focus on yourself.

If you feel insecure, then quit fussing, conjure up whatever you think you're missing as best as you can and start contributing something other than nay saying bullshit. If you don't think you're a naysayer, then start listening to how you talk to yourself in your own head and then you'll know for sure. You *do* have the power to create what you want to as long as you are strong enough to say yes to yourself. Once you start saying yes to yourself you'll let go of saying no to other people.

Maybe one reason why so many people are afraid or hesitant to come out with what they really want is that there was so much incredible material in the 20th century. There were so many enduring legacies to draw from that perhaps my generation feels too much pressure to continue. There is pressure, but that's nothing to be afraid of. We spend so much time comparing ourselves to other people in the history books and in our daily lives that we forget to do the most important thing, which is just to live your own dream. Maybe we should focus a little less on being perfectionists and focus a little more on not being afraid of our own creativity and where it leads us. If we edit and re-edit and re-edit our own ideas, they may get better but they may also get worse. There comes a point when the drawing board won't help you anymore. What will help you is life experience, going out and trying your ideas. Put your idea to the test. See how it goes.

In music, we have a wonderful advantage. All we're doing is moving air. We can't hurt anybody with music. We're not doing surgery or building rockets. Leave that kind of stress to them. Come out with it already. Don't hide. Don't shy away from what you really want to do. Don't shy away from *yourself*. If you've been on a certain path don't be afraid to change it. If you have to convince yourself that you like your life just the way it is, that's a good sign that you should change it. The past doesn't matter. What you did yesterday doesn't matter. What you're "known for" doesn't matter. What does matter is that you go and live your life the way you want to because as far as we know you only have one. *You're ready.*

Every day you take a step forward. Make sure it's in the direction that you truly want to go in, in your heart of hearts. Don't waste your life trying to fulfill the goals of yesterday if today's goals are different. Every

144

day we make choices. If you want to change your life you have to change something that you are doing every day, because life is made up of single days. If the details don't change, the big picture does not change. Someone once said, "There are seven days in a week and someday isn't one of them," so get moving. The motivational speaker Robin Sharma couldn't have put it better. "Change is hard at the beginning, messy in the middle and gorgeous at the end."

:‖ 26 ‖:

Dare to Dream

"You just do it. You force yourself to get up. You force yourself to put one foot before the other, and God damn it, you refuse to let it get to you. You fight. You cry. You curse. Then you go about the business of living. That's how I've done it. There's no other way."

— Elizabeth Taylor

"**D**are to Dream." I used to think that phrase was cliché and really pretty obvious. Of course we should all "dare" to dream. But what does that actually mean? Daring to dream is indeed a dare. It takes courage and a lot of inner strength and self-love. You must dare to visualize, in space and time, your deepest and brightest dreams. I'm not talking about dreams of becoming wealthy or finally getting the car you want or anything like that. I'm talking about the dreams that are so sacred to you that you don't even tell anyone about them, dreams that seem impossible. I'm talking about the kind of dreams that most people who are already on a creative, difficult, rare or prestigious path sometimes don't unleash into their own minds because the new dream would throw a big wrench into the whole thing.

Why aren't people honest with themselves about their dreams? Here's why. If you truly let those visualizations into your mind, and furthermore, if you start to believe that they could *actually happen,* you could risk being burdened with the lifelong task of making them happen. You may want something so magnificent, so strange, so unbelievably "not you" seeming that you've never actually tried to visualize the truth which is this: What you want, on the deepest and brightest level, really is possible.

Why is it so hard for us to allow ourselves the chance to imagine reaching our highest, most profound potential, the thing that would make us the happiest? It's because throughout life, we've created identities for ourselves made up of where we come from, what people say to us, what our current talents and skills are, where we went to school, what we think other people think about us, how much money we make, and it goes on and on. Instead of providing a reliable, sturdy self image, this so-called identity also known as the ego actually holds us back and creates endless delusions about everything in life, especially our own potential.

Daring to dream is like opening a Pandora's box. For a moment, when you open that box in your mind, you can ask, "What If?" That "What If?" question can be incredibly powerful. But once the answer rushes out at you, you have to be ready to face it head on and chase it down. You can't think to yourself, "Oh, I'm not good enough for that. I could never get there," or, "But I'm not the right kind of person to do that kind of thing," or "I'm not pretty enough or hard working enough," or, "What will my friends or family think?" or my personal favorite, "…but I already have such a good thing going here doing this thing and I don't want to change my path. I like my path I'm good at it and it's worked out for me so far."

Well, there's a saying that goes along with this, and it used to really piss me off until I dared to dream: You have to give up the good to get the great. That means that you have to leave your comfort zone, leave your safe spot, your easy job, or your already well-developed talent in order to go on a new adventure. Maybe it's not a totally new adventure, but a new component to the adventure, or maybe it's a new way of doing the adventure, or maybe it's a new style, a new medium or a new skill to add. Whatever it may be, when you dare to dream, get ready to have the shit scared right out of you, because like it or not, your dreams are never wrong about you. A dream will never pick the wrong person to have it.

If you find yourself daydreaming from time to time imagining a new idea or journey for yourself and saying, "Nahhhh, that couldn't happen to me," then wake up and smell the denial! Don't avoid your ideas and pretend that they don't exist. Don't reinforce your current situation by saying things like, "No, I don't do that, I only do *this*." Here's another profound truth. "It's not what you are that that holds you back, it's what you think you're not that does." It even happened to me. Everyone asked why I didn't sing and I always said very confidently, "Well I don't sing. I play the violin and that's it. That's all. I'm happy with the violin and you should be too!" And guess what I ended up doing a few weeks later?

The same thing happened with song writing. I didn't like the idea of being a "song writer." I didn't like the idea of being any of the things I was becoming. I was too attached to the ego's negative judgment about the terms "jazz violinist" and "singer/ songwriter" and so on and so forth. As soon as I labeled what I was doing, I didn't like the sound of it. And that's because as soon as you try to capture a creative concept with words, the words usually remove its true essence. I was feeling trapped by stereotypes and clichés and believed that I *was* a stereotype and a cliché.

Eventually I remembered that who I am is not just a word or a phrase. Who I am is me. I felt at times like I didn't fit in, like I was too weird or unusual or like I'd become "just another so and so..." and it had really worn me down. I had trapped myself with these concepts. I'm not a concept. I'm a person, and so are you.

While I'm being honest, I don't think I would have had such an interest in singing or writing songs if I had made great money playing jazz violin from the beginning. I felt that I needed to add more to my albums and my shows to get more people to connect with the music. Maybe the fact that I had struggled with my identity and to make better money was a good thing. I stopped judging myself based on these concepts that have nothing to do with my real life, and I became a more free and confident performer. I dared to dream, and it was hard at first, but it was worth it. I just pushed all of that doubt off of a cliff.

After I hung up a lot of my hang-ups I asked myself, *OK, you wanna write songs? What kind of music do you like to listen to?* That's where I started. Every time I think about writing a song, even if it's just a tune for the band to play with no words, I always start by thinking of what I like to listen to the most and use that as inspiration. If I don't want to hear it then why would I play it?

I started to see my life in music as a bouquet of flowers. I had a good bunch of red roses and that was swing. I love red roses and think that having a bouquet of just one kind of flower is beautiful, but I started to wonder if I wanted to add more types of flowers to my bouquet. I added some new colors, petals of new sizes and textures and shapes, maybe some other plants that weren't flowers at all. *That's* the kind of bouquet I like to have now, but the roses are still in there.

Daring to dream also opens up the possibility for your dreams to change over time, either in big or small ways. The point of daring to dream is not that you get in touch with your truest dreams once and then your whole life path is set. The point is that by daring to dream, you're able to be honest with yourself without interference from the ego and all of the false limitations it reminds you of. You've resolved to stay on the path that's not falsely limited, however changing and evolving it may be.

It's a way of maintaining your relationship with your true self so you don't lose your way. If your taste changes, that's fine. If it doesn't, that's fine too, but daring to dream is a great way to always keep a good strong hold on what you want in your heart of hearts. There's no lying there, no cover-ups, no excuses, no scheming to ignore your vision, no convincing yourself that you're happy "enough" with what you already have. There is just pure intention, pure unfiltered possibility, waiting for you to believe in it.

We also must remember to dare to dream because there are billions of people on Earth who are born into war, famine, poverty, abuse and other devastation that they cannot control who don't have the possibility to follow their dreams. We must not waste our capacity to dream and our privilege to follow our dreams once we allow them to inspire us. And, hopefully, your dreams will lead you to help as many people in need around the world as possible. This is certainly a dream of mine.

:| 27 |:

Authenticity

"Just don't give up trying to do what you really want to do. Where there is love and inspiration, I don't think you can go wrong."

– Ella Fitzgerald

A friend asked me recently why some art seems more authentic when presented by one artist and much less authentic when "copied" by another. And, given the nature of all art being borrowed and stolen, passed down and constantly recycled from artist to artist, where does true integrity lie? How do you know what's real? The answer, in my opinion, goes back to fear and daring to dream.

Artists that come off phony are artists that are creating or borrowing ideas out of fear. They feel insecure and that they need something outside of themselves to make them popular enough, wealthy enough or commercial enough. You can usually bet that if someone doesn't seem authentic, it's probably because that person is motivated by fear. When the art comes from within you, you're not afraid. When the art comes from outside of you, you're afraid. You're just clinging to something. You can't embody it if you're clinging to it.

How can we not be motivated by fear? By daring to dream. In that state we are able to see what we really want to do as opposed to seeing who we want to be in the vision of someone else, or what we want people to think about us or who we are trying to sell tickets to. Believe it or not, getting rid of fear doesn't really have all that much to do with originality, either. It has more to do with love than anything. It may seem counter intuitive, but let me explain.

How can a great classical violinist play 250-year-old music and sound authentic? How can a jazz musician play 80-year-old songs and sound authentic? These songs have gone through thousands of renditions and their performances have been borrowed and stolen even more times. It comes down to the intention of the artist. That is where the integrity and the authenticity come from.

The artist must truly and deeply want and love to do what he or she is doing for it to come across authentically. If the artist is creating out of fear primarily then it will be phony nearly every time. Think of the children of famous people who try to emulate their well-known parents and often fail because they seem insincere. It's because they are afraid to not live up to their parents, or that they'll look unworthy of being related to their own parents, or they're afraid to pay an homage because they don't want to screw it up, or they're afraid to do their own thing and to receive criticism on why they didn't pay an homage, and so on and so forth. If they had just let go of that fear then things would be much easier.

Of course, there are classical violinists that are totally inauthentic and there are jazz musicians that are as phony as can be, but that's because in those cases, the artists don't want to be doing what they are doing or they want it for an inauthentic reason. They would likely rather be doing something else, and if that's true, they should do something else!

Music can be brand new or passed down hundreds of times, but either way, whether it comes off as authentic or phony depends on if the performer believes deeply in what he or she is doing or not. There is no substitute for loving what *you do* and how *you do* it. You can only discover what you love and how you want to do it by daring to dream.

That doesn't mean you shouldn't steal an idea from someone. Of course you should if you want to, but always remember *why* you are using that specific idea. If you really believe in it, if it is part of your soul, if you love it not because of the person or era it's attached to, but because you believe that this idea is a part of your own true vision, then whatever you've stolen or borrowed will strengthen your authenticity. For example, Jimi Hendrix influenced Prince, but playing the guitar like Jimi made Prince stronger as an artist, because Prince believed in it and it was part of his *ultimate and original* vision. Prince didn't do it because he thought it'd be good for the producers or anything like that. He loved to play the guitar (somewhat) like Jimi, so that's what he did.

On the contrary, if you want to use someone else's idea because you feel that you need it to reinforce something that you don't truly have on your own or because you're afraid that without it your identity is in jeopardy, or that you need it to cover up some other type of insecurity, then it'll probably have a negative effect on your art. All in all, it's got to be about being yourself! Your ultimate and original vision has to come from within *you*, not a record company, not a marketing strategist, not anyplace but you. Choose what you want to do out of love, not fear, and embody the truth and the liveliness of your vision with every cell of your body. That is the way to being real.

This is the reason that some artists, even ones who are talented, intelligent and friendly, feel totally inauthentic except to certain fans who are usually completely ignorant about that art form or whose taste is... *questionable.* Artists of this sort, the charlatan we'll call it, are usually operating out of some sort of fear or insecurity, but it is buried deep and strategically masked with a *false* identity, which is the one that the public sees. This kind of charlatan or spectacle artist usually does what I call "capitalizing on ignorance," which means that the artist continues to have success as long as the audience is ignorant about the art form and about what makes someone truly real and authentic.

The opposite of capitalizing on ignorance is capitalizing on enrichment. That means the artist's success continues to grow the more he or she is able to enlighten and enrich the audience by eliminating ignorance about that art form. Also the artist will come out with higher and higher quality performances, perpetually elevating the audience's (and culture's) taste. Put simply, you can become famous by spreading ignorance or by spreading enrichment. I know which team I'm on.

This also relates to why I think elderly people should keep playing in public as long as they are able and willing. In general, the more experience you have, the less you are affected or distorted by insecurity. Elderly musicians aren't worried about the same stuff younger musicians worry about because they've been along for such a long time. Old folks tend to have more depth, wisdom, patience, higher self-esteem, and a greater sense of gratitude. They may not be as energetic or experimental as the young folks, but they don't fall into the same phony habits and worries either.

Sometimes when I meet an older musician, someone who really plays well, someone who had an abundant and long lasting career, who has a beautiful tone and a wonderful touch, and that person tells me that he or she hardly plays at all anymore, it breaks my heart. The older you are, the more you should play, as long as the body and spirit allow. The older you are, the more the world needs to hear you. It's hard to come by the kind of depth and wisdom that only old age can bring a musician. You can hear it in all of the greats that kept at it long after they could have retired, like Clark Terry, Tony Bennett, B.B. King, Stéphane Grappelli, Sonny Rollins, Oscar Peterson and Ella Fitzgerald.

Sometimes the opposite is the case, too. Sometimes the earlier work of an artist seems to be better and more authentic than the later or newer work. In the beginning we're motivated by passion. Blood sweat and tears and raw creativity push us forward while we work in an often undesirable workspace with very limited resources. This causes some artists to take more risks and to pay attention more closely to following their original goals and inspirations. Also, earlier on in an artistic career, you're closer to why you started doing it in the first place. You're closer to the original flame. The car is barely running so you steer it with your hands firmly on the wheel.

As time goes on and external factors like criticism and outside influence start to shape and sometimes distort your perception of your work or the work itself, months and even years go by without remembering why you started doing what you wanted to do in the first place. You've lost your focus and your taste. The car is moving fast and driving itself. Once control is lost, it's easy to get it back provided you're willing to take an honest, straightforward look at who you truly are.

:| 28 |:

The Real McCoy

"A musicologist is a man who can read music but can't hear it."

— *Thomas Beecham*

Being the best in the world is not a very important goal compared to the goal of being the best you that you can be. The only reason that being the best in the world is considered an achievement is that in comparison to others, it's true. In fact, there can never be one true champion at anything but that's another subject. When you break out of comparison and focus on being the best that you can be, you're freeing yourself not only to be the full you, the full creative you which may be something that no one has ever done or seen before. You're also freeing yourself of the burden of comparing your talent and progress to someone else's talent and progress, which can very quickly drive you crazy.

The only thing that matters is how good you are at expressing yourself and your vision. When you stop trying to be the best in the world and start trying to be the best you can be, you no longer feel chained to what people will think of you, how people judge the type of music you make or the people you hang out with, and you don't have to fit the physical, psychological, cultural mold of "The Person Who is the Best in the World at What I do." You don't have to be what people are expecting. You don't even have to be what *you're* expecting. You are not the wrong person for the job of being your most complete self! You are the right person for it and you are the only person for it. And if you haven't realized it already, then realizing it may only require just a small adjustment in your thinking. Don't worry about what anyone else is doing. Worry about what you're doing. That's the way to be free.

Along with freeing yourself from those burdens you also have a much, *much* tougher job. It's a trade-off, really. It is both freeing and terrifying at the same time. With great power comes great responsibility. Why is this freeing and terrifying? Now you will need to be honest about where your passions lead you. It goes back once again to daring to dream. You will have to let go of who you thought you were and who you thought you would become if much of that was tied to this narrow minded role of "the best _____ in the world" which you were trying to fulfill.

You have a tougher and much more enriching journey now, which is one with no limitations, no shoes to fill, no torch to pass, no responsibility to be or do anything, not if you don't want that. You have to dig deep and be brave. Sometimes in order to get to the bottom of your passion and your creativity you have to do things that scare the flipping life out of you. Evolution is gradual. It's painful, and it's scary. I'm in the middle of all of this myself and that's why I wrote this book in the first place. Every time you jump off that cliff, you're getting closer and closer to *the real you*. And being the real you, truly embodying that, really is the best feeling in the world.

You've got to be the real mccoy even when there's bullshit all around you. It's true that these days, extraordinary things don't happen in the music industry as much anymore. The fairytale of going on TV to do a talk show or an opera and having a record contract and a world tour waiting for you the following week is basically over. Why is it over? Most of the variables that made that kind of stuff possible are all out of the equation. Take the example I just gave you. First, you'd need a show that broadcasts high-level artistic content like a world-class jazz, symphony orchestra or opera performance or something like that. That doesn't happen very much. Then, you'd need a lot of people to be watching it (and not whatever other garbage is on TV), so that the network or producers or whoever would know how well received it was by the general public. That doesn't happen either. You'd need money to produce the show, network, etc. and to pay the performers and the crew well, so that there was competition to be on these kinds of shows in the first place, and that the people on them were truly the best of the best. Without money, the best of the best go elsewhere where they can find money. Then you'd need record labels with money and a desire to invest in high-level art (very rare), and finally there'd have to be a global audience (most people don't want to leave their houses and buy a ticket anymore because of the internet), venues and of course media to cover high-level artists in a mainstream way (also very rare). That's just the beginning of it really.

There are innumerable variables that in the past helped to propel artists to the kind of worldwide success they deserved and worked for, but many of them have up and left. They quit making, supporting, funding, broadcasting and writing about great art so now it's up to the artists. It's a shame that it's like this. There's so much pressure put on artists now. We have to do so much ourselves. We have to do a million jobs before we even think about working on what we're really meant to be working on – our art! Record companies just aren't interested in doing anything besides making money, and as long as I'm on this subject, I think that real art and real talent *can* make money and a lot of it! As long as the only goal is to make money then that's all they're going to make. I hope that going forward, we can all realize the need for great art in the world, and we can also realize that if we want to make money, as long as that's not the only thing we want to do, that we can make great art and be prosperous, even very prosperous, at the same time.

Unfortunately, the general public has a very skewed vision of what it's like to be a young person trying to make it as an artist. They think that if you're associated with a celebrity that you're making huge sums of money, or if you're appearing on TV or have thousands of fans online that you're making huge sums of money. Many years ago this may have been the case, but there are numerous variables that once provided a good standard of living for young artists that don't exist anymore even for the best of the best of us.

For example, going on tour with a major star used to pay several times more than it does now. Record labels and other companies are forced to squeeze every last penny out of a tour to make it profitable, as record sales don't provide the kind of revenue they're looking for. So what do they do? They cut the paycheck of the band and the dancers and the crew and spend more money on marketing or whatever will get more people to the shows. There used to be a powerful union for musicians, but it doesn't hold much water now, especially when you compare it to the unions for actors and other artists in the film industry. Almost all the gigs for musicians are non-union, so they can pay the musicians as little as they want to. A lot of venues don't way to pay bands to play when they can hire a DJ for half the cost, or stream music from Spotify for free. It goes on and on.

Let's get back to the real mccoy. We know that most of the art that's meant for mainstream enjoyment is controlled by artless corporate interests with no integrity or taste whatsoever. What artists need to do is be the real mccoy even when we are catapulted to success, even when there is a lot of money to be made and a lot of media coverage. We still have an opportunity to do great, beautiful and lasting things in the face of this tremendous corporate machine.

I know what you're thinking. The general public doesn't want to see high art. They're ignorant, and they want garbage. I disagree. I think they would like to see higher quality entertainment if they were exposed to it more often. We've got to get people in front of great art in bigger numbers. We have to elevate their taste and experience. We have to reinvigorate the general public's love for live music, for quality performances and for real talent. The great museums of the world always have a line out the door. That's because the global public knows how important these paintings and sculptures are. We must create a respect and love for all art forms that is strong and unwavering, and we must try our best to create work that is worthy of that respect and love for generations to come. The word "artist" is used too frequently. True artists *do* create work that is worthy of deep and lasting respect. A phony artist makes work to be thrown away.

Don't compromise what you've worked for because of whom you are working for. Take the focus off of Hollywood. We've seen enough weapons, sex, money, war, glamour, wealth, gossiping and materialism. Put the focus back on art, on music, on peace, education, unity, the environment, science, intellect, adventure and personal development. In other words, don't use art to make money. Use the money to make art.

Don't let integrity escape *your* equation when and if you find yourself in a position of attention, wealth, fame and power. This is the responsibility of today's mainstream artists. Remember that your talent will never leave you. It can only leave you if you walk away first.

:‖ 29 ‖:

Yes People

"Always bear in mind that your own resolution to succeed is more important than any other."

— Abraham Lincoln

One of the first steps to getting what you want in life is to say yes to it. If you really start analyzing your own thoughts, you may be surprised how often you wish for things but after you wish for them you add a negative prediction. "I want this but could never get there," or "It would be so great if I could do that but there's no way I'll ever work that hard," or "I dream of this idea but I'm too lazy." Well the first thing you have to do is stop saying no and start saying yes. Negativity keeps you down. Yes will bring you up.

When you ask yourself, "Can I be this great?" or "Can I be this beautiful?" Say to yourself, *hell yeah, why not!* Make it happen. Help someone out if you can. The world needs more people to say yes. Saying yes to yourself is a high ledge to get onto but once you get onto it it's amazing. You *can* be that successful, that smart, that talented, that in love – that anything. The answer is yes. You can have it all, but first, you have to tell yourself that you can. If we can learn to say yes to our deepest and most worthy desires and yes to our goals and yes to our futures, they are much more likely to arise. If you visualize it, it will come!

By saying yes to yourself, you're committing yourself to believing in the possibility that maybe, just maybe, you could be right. How will you ever get anything that you want if you never believe that you could be right?

We must say yes to ourselves but also yes to one another if possible. The world's yes people make it go round. Yes people are people who aren't afraid to do something right the first time. They're not afraid to make something happen if it can happen. They're not afraid of risk, they're not afraid to go the extra mile just because it's inconvenient to do so, they're not afraid to do a favor for someone or help someone out. They're not afraid to pay a little extra attention or put in a little more effort because they say yes to the greatness of the outcome. Yes people are not afraid to find a way to make things happen.

Saying yes doesn't set you up to have too many expectations, either. All you're doing is saying yes to an honest try. If what you want isn't successful the first time, maybe the next time around you can say yes to a second try, or maybe an 82nd try. All you're doing is saying yes to giving whatever it is you want a real shot. It may be a shot in the dark, but a shot is a shot. Yes people also know that there are no limits. When you say yes to trying something, you're also saying yes to going beyond it, to achieving more than you bargained for. If you throw the dart thinking you might make it near the center of the target, remember that you may hit the Bullseye!

I try my best to be a yes person when it's possible. Too many people say no when it would be just as easy to say yes. People say no just for the fun of it. I don't get it. I can remember a time recently when I was at a concert in Los Angeles. I knew the artist who was performing and he had given me a backstage pass. During the show I met two young men in the audience who were trying to get a ukulele autographed by the artist after the show but a security guard told them they couldn't bring it in. I spoke to the artist's manager and he was able to organize for the security to allow them to bring in their ukulele and to bring it backstage for the autograph. They thanked me several times, but in all honesty, it took me 2 minutes to ask the manager if he'd allow them to bring in the ukulele. It just took a moment and these people walked away with an experience and a treasure of a lifetime. That's what being a yes person is about.

The world needs more people who ask, "Alright. How can we make this work? This is a great idea." Or when you need help, someone says, "Let me see what I can do for you. I'm going to try to help you." Yes people say, "It's so crazy it just might work." Screw the protocol! We should all try to say yes to life as much as we can. Sure, plane tickets are expensive. Sure, you don't know if you're invited to the party or not. Sure, nobody's tried it before. Yes people do it anyway. Yes people show up for life and when you do that, anything is possible. Sometimes it even turns out infinitely better than you had hoped for. It can only turn out better if you allow it to turn out.

:| 30 |:

If You Feel It, It's Yours

"You have to have confidence in your ability, and then be tough enough to follow through."

— Rosalynn Carter

Oftentimes I find myself meeting people when I'm not performing and I don't have my violin with me. When I tell somebody that I'm a jazz violinist they sometimes look at me like I just told them my mother was a butterfly, or like I'm the world's leading expert on wormholes. A big "yeah right," expression comes across their face, and if not that, a nice blank "I have no idea what jazz violin is," stare comes along. I don't blame anybody for not knowing much about what it is that I do or for not believing that someone who looks like me could be good at it, but that doesn't make it any less tiring to overcome.

For years I've tried to focus on strengthening the qualities that make up a real musician like playing something well in one take, having a nice sound, moving an audience with a melody and being professional. I don't think many people realize just how much time and effort I've put into practicing and refining the skills needed to perform and record on a high level.

Some people have accused me of being not very creative, of not being a true artist. It's amazing that some people don't see playing jazz as creative when we improvise 80% of the time we're on stage *and in the recording studio*, but they see writing the same song with three chords in 20 different ways as creative. Of course, they are both creative in different ways, but improvisation is no doubt the epitome of creativity in my opinion. Would the same people look Ella Fitzgerald or Oscar Peterson in the eye and accuse them of not being "true artists?" I don't think so.

What I believe some people fail to see is that I've cultivated a lot of skills that most musicians in my generation don't have, skills that I believe the majority of today's mainstream musical artists also don't have. Nobody sees how hard you have worked when all they see is how you look. I know other artists that feel the same way. You just have to make people believe you. It's a shame that the artists who are the top in terms of quality are not the top in terms of popularity, resources, financial success, support or recognition, but I think that someday it'll change. People can only take in so much garbage for so long. You have to know how important you are. You have to know it and you have to prove it, even if nobody cares but you.

I remember one time when I had booked a gig at a small venue in London. The venue told me that they wanted to hire musicians for me who I didn't know and I hadn't heard before. I'd told them beforehand that I wanted to hire the band myself but they didn't listen. Maybe they didn't listen because I was young or because I played the violin or because I was female. Who knows.

They reassured me that they would find musicians "suitable" for me and that I shouldn't worry about their level of playing. Then what happens? The gig starts and I'm not able to play my best because they frankly weren't up to it musically. There's a lesson right there. People will underestimate you left and right unless you take the matter into your own hands. It can be tiresome. I've been told by club owners that they'll give me my own date but only if the entire band is female. How would men like it if we told them what gender their band mates had to be? They'd like it fine if they had to be men, and not because men are better musicians. It's because there are by far way more male musicians to choose from. So this is what some of us are up against.

There were other times at jam sessions or gigs that I wasn't allowed to play because someone else who played violin who was older than me was playing and he or she couldn't play as well as I could. Everyone knew that and didn't want me to hurt that person's feelings. Because of situations like that, there have been times that I've had to sit on the sidelines listening to BS instead of being included. Unbelievable. I'll *never* do that to a young person. I'll never exclude someone from learning something and sharing their gift with the audience just to spare someone's ego. It's so backwards when people do that.

Thank goodness it doesn't always go that way. The other day after I played a concert with about eight older jazz musicians someone mentioned to me that I look like I'm in a lion's den. I'm often surrounded by a handful of men on stage, at least a foot taller than me, most of them old enough to be my grandfathers. When I walk on stage it seems to me that the audience is often wondering what the heck kind of business I have playing with these people, on a violin no less! Maybe I'm someone's daughter or girlfriend, maybe someone lost a bet. Who knows.

People have told me that from playing my first note, the audience changes from having an expression that says, "What is this about?" to something completely different. And sometimes, if I'm performing with people I don't know, the musicians on stage change their expressions right away too. But what is that?

I'll tell you what it is. It's the realization that nobody owns anything. Nobody owns any styles, any licks, any repertoire, any anything. If you feel it, then you can play it. There's no reason to think that you shouldn't express yourself however you want to. If you want to learn the creativity and artistry of another culture, then study it. *Don't be weak in your self-expression because you fear that your physical appearance doesn't support someone's small-minded assumptions about it.* If you feel it, it's authentic. If you feel it, it's yours. Don't make it easier for people to judge you. Make it impossible.

If you want to sing the blues, then sing the blues. Don't just sing this way or that way because of what you look like. Nobody cares what you look like. Nobody cares what race you are or how tall or short you are or what kind of clothes you wear or what kind of an accent you have. When you sing what you want to sing, or play what you want to play, it'll hit people in the heart and hearts don't have eyes. So stop giving a crap about what you look like and whether or not it matches your creative calling. *Be yourself.* Look how you want to look. Be who you want to be. If people look at you like, "who does she think she is?" Just respond in your own mind, "I'll tell you who I think I am! I'm going to do it right now!"

This may be obvious to some people, but the reality is that many performers who don't fit the stereotype of their performance role face a tremendous amount of judgment from audiences and fellow performers on a daily basis. The best ones put that to rest as soon as the first note comes out, but on the next night, it's the same thing again.

Well, I think it's good to shake things up. Who gives a flying flip what you look like? What does it matter if you look like the typical version of whatever it is you're trying to do or be? This is where being your best self comes in really handy. If you're being your best self, there is no history. There is no preconceived idea about who you are or what the proper way to do anything is. It's just you and your life. It's enormously freeing. I see every day, in every venue, in every college, there are musicians and young creatives who are jaded, diluted, confused, and losing hope. What they need is to realize very deeply what they want in life and to remove any fear on the path to getting there. Period.

People invent new ways of performing all the time and the public accepts them because the performance exudes authentic human expression. Some genius will come along and sell millions of albums doing something slightly left of center like mixing genres, burning a guitar on stage, acting up a new stage persona, pioneering a new style of dance or a new technology. At first when it comes out I'm sure that person receives a lot of negative criticism. People will say it's too much of this thing or too much of that thing. Look at Lady Gaga. She faced years of discouragement because people thought she was "too theater" and now we totally accept her. She combines a wide variety of musical and artistic styles and still manages to be herself because it's all flowing through her. She stopped trying to be the best in the world and tried to be her best self, and look where it took her. If she had left all of that behind and just been another boring pop star, she would already be a thing of the past. But she didn't do that. She wanted more.

Anybody can be anything, so don't be afraid to be what you want to be. Be afraid that you're holding back. As soon as you let go, there is truly nothing standing in your way. There are no judgments; there are no worries about how things will be received. Screw it! If you feel it, it's yours. Don't be immature. Your art isn't interested in immaturity. Just jump on the train.

I've changed my style and my creative goals many times, and I'm sure they'll keep changing and evolving as I get older. That's art. We have to follow where our inspiration takes us, not our egos or our pre-determined audiences. Most of the songs I've written came to me out of thin air. The form, the chords, the melody and the lyrics all came to me at once. All I had to do was open my mouth and out it came. You have to accept what is coming to you. All I know is that when you feel excited about something, no matter what it is, you've gotta answer the door.

:‖ 31 ‖:

It's a Man's World

"The woman who can create her own job is the woman who will win fame and fortune."

– Amelia Earhart

Even in this early stage in my life I've experienced a tremendous amount of bullshit from men in the music industry. I know it's tough for women everywhere, especially ones who are both beautiful and sharp, to get the kind of respect, acknowledgement and work they deserve. We see it all of the time. Why aren't there more women in political office or in science fields or playing in bands?

The truth is if you're beautiful and sharp, some men, the ones I'm talking about, are going to feel a contradicting way about you. They shouldn't, but some men are children. They respect you and are attracted to you at the same time, which makes them feel threatened by you and want to seduce you. That creates a situation in which men will put you down and hit on you at the same time. They want to control you because your intelligence is threatening to them, but they want to have sexual power over you because you're beautiful. It happens to young women in every field.

Of course some men give up on working with smart women and just hire them based on their looks. They'd rather women not complicate things with talent and intelligence, so they just stop looking for it, or ignore it even if it's there. If they have to work with women, they might as well work with beautiful ones and forget about talent. It's absurd. I won't tell you anyone's name because if I did, they would be firstly mortified and secondly, would lie, deny, and make excuses. Also, since some of these men are quite well known, you probably wouldn't believe me anyway.

There are a few variations on this, but it always happens more or less the same way. The man tells the woman that he respects her, wants to be friends and that he wants to work together or something like that. It all seems professional, respectful and lovely. Then, as soon as there is an opportunity to ask about a boyfriend or to take advantage of that professional or platonic relationship, a man will do that.

It's easy to see how some women feel that their intelligence, their talent and their expertise is being undermined by the selfishness of the man. So when women are given opportunities by men and the men think that it's fine to do this "put you down/ try to get you to sleep with me" thing, women feel not only used, but that their intellect is basically worthless. Now I'm not talking about men who really fall in love with women they work with. I'm talking about men who disrespect and manipulate women so that they can check them off of their weekly conquest list. Perhaps they just want to see what they can get away with. Either way, it's disgusting.

To me, this is why so many women have all but given up on being true forces of nature in the world. Sexual harassment is rampant. Plenty of women have tremendous talent and potential but they don't use it because of the way men make them feel. They'll hit on you and demean you at the same time so what's the point? They won't pay you as much as the men either, and if you refuse their advances they'll fire you. It's a disgrace.

I've been in recording sessions for my own albums and have heard Grammy-winning engineers make jokes about me filming pornography into the microphone for everyone in the studio to hear. I've had Academy Award winning film composers tell me that they'd like me to lose weight before performing with them so that, "I can look sexier like Lady Gaga or Madonna." I didn't mention their awards because I care about the awards themselves. I'm just trying to make you see how prevalent this is, even among "professionals."

Drunk musicians have asked me to marry them at gigs. Record company executives have sexually harassed me. People working in the recording studio have tried to kiss me and then tell me I'm not allowed to tell anyone else that they tried. I've had friends try to physically restrain me from leaving the room when I didn't go along with their idea of a nice evening with me. I've been introduced as the "sex symbol" for the band in front of an audience. I've been thrown into very compromising situations with men behind a closed door, and when I told my friends about it they blamed me or called me a liar. It's endless. And I've had it pretty easy compared to many women.

I won't tell you which one of my university professors held this opinion, but when I brought it up to him that the young men in the jazz program were harassing the young women to an unacceptable degree, he called me a drama queen and told me that I was seeing what I wanted to see. He had no idea what I was talking about, but it was a real problem. I was speaking up about something the other young women were afraid to mention and I was being totally ignored. Of course things never changed. That was just the way it was.

Sometimes there is genuine attraction between two people. In that case, I would hope that the man would ask the woman about how she felt and that whatever her response may be, he would respect it. Sometimes, unfortunately, men don't listen to women when they turn them down. Sometimes it's because they're under the influence, they think the women are playing hard to get, or they think they can change the woman's mind. *That* kind of behavior has got to stop. It also happens that when a woman doesn't agree to go out with a man or to sleep with him, she will not only lose a friend but will be fired. That's happened to me, too.

While I'm on this subject, it's a huge problem that in the entertainment world and well beyond, women get assaulted, harassed, even raped and abused, and then will find a way to blame themselves for what's happened. I've seen it happen to women I've known over and over again, and the real problem is that many women and a lot of men don't know when it is happening. They think sexual assault means rape, so they don't want to use that phrase, "sexual assault." I've heard men make excuses for their friends or one another when horrible things happen because they're just so ignorant about the concept of consent, the law, and the frequency of these kinds of incidents. If there is no consent then it is sexual assault. That is the law. It doesn't mean there is a fight or a screaming argument or the man has to physically injure the woman. It still is assault.

Many women (and men) don't know that no matter what you're wearing or how much you've had to drink that when a man assaults or harasses you it's not your fault. Women don't know that they aren't supposed to need to defend themselves around men in fear that something like this could happen. It's not right. It gets worse, unfortunately. When this kind of thing in any degree happens to a woman, especially in the entertainment business, women don't have anywhere to turn.

As Vice President Joe Biden has said, it is time to end the notion that an institution or individual's reputation is more valuable than safety and justice for victims of sexual assault and in some cases, rape.

If women start calling men out for what they're doing, half of the industry will go to court. That is one possible answer, but is not likely to happen. The answer is that men have got to stop sexually assaulting and raping women.

Most women do nothing when they are assaulted or raped because they don't know how to defend themselves against people who either don't know the law or won't own up to what they did. Society often blames the woman for what happened or the perpetrator may have the financial or professional power to ruin someone's career for telling the truth. It's disgusting. I've seen a lot of women who are even afraid to tell their families or their friends because deep down, they feel some sense of responsibility, guilt or shame for what happened. They feel at fault so much that they can't even tell the truth.

If it's someone well known who has done this to you, and in the entertainment world it usually is, you could tell the press if you want it to be publically known (not very attractive to most women), you could tell the police and get the person who did this to you involved which could cost you your career and a lot of respect (not to mention many people involved may accuse you of lying), you could talk directly to the man or his friends and that would cost you relationships and respect (if they even believe what you said or agree with what you're accusing him of), or, you can keep quiet about it, do nothing, and move on.

The first time I was sexually assaulted was at a party in my hometown, five minutes away from my house. I was about 16 and I was visiting over the summer from boarding school. I got drunk and in retrospect I know that someone had drugged my drink. The whole night was a blur of semi-conscious confusion, which ended when I found myself with my clothes on inside out in the back yard of my friend's house vomiting in the grass. Another friend at the party found me and took me home. I told my parents what had happened and they didn't seem to believe me. My boyfriend at the time accused me of cheating. I went back to boarding school about week later.

There have been other incidents on the road or with other musicians who I knew and respected. Once I found myself on tour with a friend and without wanting it to happen I found myself physically resisting him taking my clothes off in his hotel room. I pushed him off of me several times as hard as I could until finally I was able to leave. You could say that he and I are still friends.

Another time, I met a friend in Los Angeles for drinks after one of his performances. We were with a group of some very well known musicians. My so called friend convinced me to go up to his room for a cup of tea and I agreed, making it clear that I didn't want anything more than the tea and that I'd be leaving right after. He found a way to take most of his clothes off, locked the door and tried to kiss me while keeping one hand on the lock so that I couldn't get it out. I was backed into a corner and had to use all of my physical strength to pry him off of me and to leave his room with any dignity at all. A few nights later I told another friend what had happened and he blamed me. The stories go on and on and on and on.

Whether you're a man or a woman or transgender or any human being, you have the right to be treated with respect and dignity, and that's what we have got to promote and stand up for all over the world. We must stand up for consent and for moral and just behavior regardless of how much money or fame the perpetrator has, what time of night it is, what the victim is wearing or saying or any other circumstances that my *suggest* consent but are *not* consent.

Many of these situations aren't totally black and white. Some of them are but many of them are not. Usually, if you're even asking yourself if it was black and white, it was. Sometimes you have to retrace yours steps to see just what in the hell went so wrong. Oftentimes what is discovered is that the man didn't ask for consent and rather just assumed consent, and that is a problem. If women aren't given the chance to say no, there are men who will take the absence of an answer as a yes. That is why so many men don't even ask women before crossing an un-crossable line. They are afraid of rejection. They'd rather force themselves on you than watch you say no. They'd rather ask for forgiveness than permission.

It's a shame that so many of us feel the heavy weight of a culture that forces women to feel guilty when we don't want to grant a man's wish. We're made to feel that our non-compliance is the reason for our own pain rather than seeing that the man's lack of judgment and respect are truly the forces to blame.

But here is the bigger point – we live in a misogynistic society that pressures women to be docile, agreeable, beautiful, easy going, sexy, only mildly intelligent, and of course to be smiling all of the time. Well nobody acts this way naturally and everyone, man or woman, should be allowed to have an opinion and a full range of emotional and intellectual viewpoints. But when women are being forced to appease men because it looks "bad" for women to act as naturally and boldly as men do, I think it would be easy for a man, a stupid one, to confuse *that* social construct with genuine attraction between two people. But oftentimes when women break out of this pattern and choose to act like themselves, they lose their professional opportunities and are called cold or harsh or difficult at the same time that men would be called pragmatic and natural-born leaders.

It's horrible to be ignored or put down for simply not acting in exactly the way many people believe women should act. I've been *talked at* many times by both men and women who barely know me, who accuse me of all sorts of things. Sometimes they say, "I heard you never smile. You don't ever smile, do you?" Or "I think it's funny the way you ignore people. You're a real b**** and I guess some guys like that in a woman." Or "How come you hate me? You look like you don't like anybody." Club owners don't believe I'm a musician. People in the band don't even believe I'm a musician. It's incredible. A man once told me he thought my violin was "a large purse," or sometimes people think I'm carrying it for someone else. You can't make this stuff up, people.

Well I don't think it's very wise to make an assumption about some-one else, a negative assumption no less, and then expect for that person to enjoy your company. I try to refrain from making any assumptions about anyone. I try to give everyone the benefit of the doubt and to not pass any judgment or make any conclusions about anybody. It doesn't make other people feel very comfortable and frankly, it's not a kind thing to do. If I want to find something out about someone, I ask a question instead of stating an assumption with a question mark at the end of it.

Obviously not all people act this way. I've worked with some wonderful men who are not only respectful of women but who outwardly support women in our independence and don't wish for us to act or look any particular way. Real men stand up for women, and I mean that politically, socially, economically, on stage or anywhere else. Women are not here to simply serve men. Some women want to do that and some women don't.

That's not to say that women should get any type of special treatment just because they are women. Women need to be prepared to work alongside men and to compete with men too. Men need to stand with women in allowing the competition to be fair, dignified and respectable.

It's hard to know when you're being taken advantage of or disrespected until you know you've been taken advantage of and disrespected and sometimes, by that time, it's too late. I try to trust my gut when it comes to these things because usually my gut is right, even if I don't believe it at first. It's also important for women to not be afraid to tell a man when something he is asking about is none of his business. I can't stand it when a sleazy man tries to find out something personal about me when I clearly have no interest in telling him.

I wish that men could just appreciate women, see us as equal, and treat us with respect if something beyond a working relationship or friendship crosses their minds. It's not just a loss for women when we encounter men over and over who effectively destroy their working relationships with women. It's a loss for the men too.

All I hope is for women and men to be able to work together in equal numbers, for equal pay, and for women to be respected and celebrated alongside and by men. I see every day that there are men who stand up for women, who invite them to work alongside them without feeling threatened and without trying to take advantage. Someday all women will feel empowered and liberated to be who they are, not what men want them to be, and it's my honest opinion that the state of the world will dramatically improve. Men have run the place for centuries and everything is chaos. I think it's time for some more women to help them out.

:| 32 |:

Abstract Findings on Practice and Performance

Artur Schnabel to Albert Einstein when, during a movement of a Mozart violin sonata, Einstein got lost. Artur said, "Albert, can't you count?"

(Historical Tale)

In the last year or so I've been falling in love all over again with the peacefulness of an hours-long stretch of practice. I love to just sit down, maybe with a metronome, maybe in front of a mirror, with whatever it is I'm working on and just go into a sort of Zen-like state of pure, concentrated focus. Practicing for me is one of the most satisfying and refreshing things I do with my time. Practicing always inspires more practicing, and while I'm playing I never wish I were doing anything else. I don't believe anything else could be as worthwhile, even if *anything else* would be more fun. Sometimes I don't have time to practice as much as I'd like, but even if I can only play for 30 or 45 minutes I feel that it makes a huge difference both on my mental and physical states.

The more I play live, the more I like the sound of the acoustic violin when it's not plugged in to an amplifier or a sound system. I sometimes play with a microphone but I really prefer to play acoustically so that the real tone of the violin comes through. When you're playing jazz it's not always possible to play acoustically because almost every instrument in the band is louder than the violin and if the violin is supposed to be the leader, there can be some challenges there. As much as possible I like to record my albums with acoustic violin as well and I think that's when I sound my best.

I don't really understand the electric violin trend going on right now. I've never played an electric violin I liked and I've never heard an electric violin that sounded better than an acoustic violin. I'd rather play a junk acoustic violin than the best electric violin any day. Electric violins are physically heavy and they sound sticky and tacky, like bubblegum. To be honest, I can see why so many violinists enjoy playing electric instruments if the reason that they do it is that they can't get a nice tone out of an acoustic violin. The electric violin is very easy to play. The more effects you add to it, the more places there are to hide, technique-wise. For me, there is nothing greater than the natural sound of a violin so I try to keep it that way as much as possible.

One thing I've learned over the years is that there is truly no substitute for hard work. It's not easy to put a musical career together. Your responsibility is not only to practice but to do a tremendous amount of work in order to create the opportunities to perform and to grow your audience. So it takes a lot of diligence and patience to make time for all of this and *still* keep practice as the main priority whenever possible. After all, that's really the job of a musician. Sometimes when I am about to get to work on something, I tell my friends, "It's time to build your future." That's what we're all doing – putting in the time and the dedication now so that we have freedom later on.

Nothing will build your future faster than working consistently, and that means sometimes working when you don't feel like it. I think that working when you don't feel like it is the definition of drive. Some people think that drive is naturally occurring in some people and not in others. Actually, drive is just the ability to see that what you want in the future is more important than what you want right now, and then to be at peace with the journey that takes you there.

It's never too late to reinvent your playing and to resolve to be better than you were yesterday. You're never too old and it's never too hard. Even if it seems nearly impossible now, if you keep working consistently and diligently, slowly and carefully, you will achieve what you want to achieve. If you put in the work and believe in yourself you can always rise to the next level. Another thing that Oprah said is that we don't become what we want. We become what we believe. We must *believe* that we'll get there.

When you practice long, hard hours you are preparing for your future. I'm not sure why it happens but when I work hard, magical things happen in life. Hard work effectively buys you the future you've dreamt of. Every minute of dedication helps to propel you towards success. Sacrifice now is success later. Restriction of freedom now is ultimate freedom later. Don't be afraid to put in the effort, no matter what it requires.

Practicing can be frustrating because to practice well, we have to come face to face with our musical and technical shortcomings. We have to analyze and observe and review them over and over very slowly and then we have to fix them with slow and steady repetition. In a sense, when you practice you are always failing. You are identifying places where you must improve and you are choosing to focus on them. But in realizing the failure, you are resolving to succeed. There's no judgment when you practice, only problem solving.

I never worry about trying to get into the right mood before I practice, because I know that once I start practicing I'll be in the right mood. Practicing puts me in a calm yet alert state. I've only had to quit practicing due to being in a bad mood a few times in my life. Usually, once I start, I just want to keep going. The best thing to get you into the mood to work is just getting to work. It may sound too simple to be true, but trust me. It's true.

When I'm practicing I always try to take it slow and let my progress evolve. I try not to overanalyze the progress I make day to day and see it as an ongoing evolutionary process instead. I also try to practice the basics as much as possible, scales and things like that, and after I'm through with that, if I even practice anything else that day, I work on a piece of music or technique that is challenging to me. Sometimes I put pieces in new keys or try an old exercise in a new way.

I try not to play anything that is easy for me because I leave that for the stage. In fact, I hardly ever practice improvisation, at least not with the same attention and focus that I practice the basics with. I focus the most on the right hand. The right hand is extremely important because it is responsible for tone, dynamics, intensity, clarity and just about every aspect of playing the violin except for intonation of the notes themselves and vibrato.

One of the most important things to do when practicing is to not simply hear yourself but to actually listen to yourself. Listen to the sound coming out of your instrument, listen to the way the notes start and end. Listen to the way that they make you feel, what kind of energy and emotion they invoke in you. Listening to yourself while you play is a difficult skill to master but it is fundamental to your ability to create the sound that you hear in your head, the sound that you are working towards.

If you're truly listening, you won't skip over a passage that you played poorly and just move on. You'll hear that you played it poorly and then you'll work to fix it. It's that simple. Every little movement, every sound, every bow change, every shift – they're all little movements that need to be controlled, calculated and listened for. I always try to move toward effortlessness. There is no "good enough" when you're practicing. Every time you try it again it should get better and better. There should be no unnecessary tension, no unnecessary movements (anywhere in the body!), just pure function and beautiful music coming out. Of course, in performance, you just walk on the stage, smile, and go. But when practicing, everything can be a constant improvement, however slow and tedious.

If I can help it, I try to not be too hard on myself. Sometimes our attention during the day is pulled in so many different directions that there's no possible way to get everything done. We have to know when to work but we also have to know when to take a break. If you overwork yourself you'll pay for it later so it's best to not overwork yourself at all. We are human beings and we can only do so much in a day, in a week and in a year. Some things take longer than we had hoped and some things require more preparation than we thought we needed. It's all part of being human. We need to trust our instincts. We need to trust ourselves and trust in letting things unfold naturally. We need to be adaptable and accepting.

In a performance the mentality is a little bit different than in practice because there is a visual and performance component to your playing that practicing doesn't involve. You must also consider entertaining the audience, putting them at ease, amazing them, playing in such a way that the whole group sounds and looks good, playing in such a way that the audience can hear and feel you, and on top of that, if you're me, you have to improvise too.

There are a few things that I've picked up that really improve the quality of a performance that don't have to do with technical details and skill at all. Smiling at the audience and looking at a few of them in the eye before you play can really improve a show. Looking like you're enjoying your performance, dressing in a way that is pleasing to them, entering and exiting the stage in a graceful way whether that means taking a bow or waving to them or whatever it is, and looking and feeling your best are all ways to tremendously improve the feeling of a show.

It's important to be comfortable when you play. If your shoes are too high or something funny is going on, your performance will suffer. You have to take care of yourself when you're going to perform. You have to drink enough water, eat something light and healthy, sleep enough the night before and get up early enough the next day. You have to feel awake. You have to feel alive. It all goes into the way you are received. The way you talk to the audience, the way you stand, how tense or loose you are, your posture, your inner space, your stage presence as a whole, is all part of the performance.

To be honest, many of the things I just mentioned were things that none of my professors in any of the schools I attended even mentioned. They were too busy talking to us about flat nine and sharp five chords that they forgot to tell people about stage presence and some of the other very important aspects of being a professional performer. Of course there are many more details that we could talk about like acoustics and lighting and so on. I'm just talking about what you as a performer can control which contributes to and defines the quality of your performance. If you smile and look happy, you're already *way* ahead of the game.

:| 33 |:

The Truth Cannot Be Destroyed

"Your need for acceptance can make you invisible in this world. Don't let anything stand in the way of the light that shines through this form. Risk being seen in all of your glory."

— Jim Carrey

In life, when you're dealing with people, it's a guarantee that you'll be misunderstood at least a few times. It's unfortunate that we can't just be seen for who we are by everyone that we encounter, but what's more important is that you know the truth about yourself no matter what anyone says or thinks about you. What you think about yourself is exactly the same as what other people think about you. You can't know what other people are thinking, so if you're wondering what other people are thinking about you, your mind will just fill in the blank with what you think about yourself. Fill in the blank with something beautiful, the truth.

If it's true for you then it's true. Nobody needs to know it's true other than you for it to be true. That doesn't mean you can say nonsense and people should believe you because you believe it. I'm talking about the truth of *who you are*. That truth cannot ever be destroyed, no matter how many people try to ignore or distort it.

It's hard when you're young. Most of the people you meet have no idea who you are, they ask you all sorts of ridiculous, small-minded questions that have nothing to do with your life and your work, and sometimes, people who have spoken to you for five minutes will claim to have "figured you out," just because you're young. Well I don't believe anyone can ever fully figure anyone else out, and in general, I like to give people the benefit of the doubt as much as possible. Like I said before, I try not to draw any concrete conclusions about anyone, because more often than not my assumptions are completely off. I wish that we could all treat each other with respect and compassion, and really give one another the benefit of the doubt no matter what happens. If someone says something nasty to me, I just let it go. Maybe that person had a bad day.

But sometimes, I find myself at the end of my rope of compassion. I just try to hang on. For instance, it really bothers me when I have to answer the same stupid questions about myself over and over to people. It can be really draining to speak to people who just have no idea who they are talking to. Sometimes when I'm asked a question about myself, the person I'm talking to doesn't even listen to my response and even more amazingly, the person sometimes doesn't even believe me.

In a sense, I don't like to be interviewed by people. I don't like when people ask me peculiar questions as if they are testing my legitimacy. I like to have real, open, honest conversations with people, the kind in which one person says something, then the other person responds and you go from there. That's a real interview and I like those. I like to ask people questions with the idea that we could become close friends, or at least that we have many things in common. I don't talk to people like I am quizzing them or looking for a place where we can disagree. I can't tell you how many times I've been in conversation and felt judged and evaluated instead of just talked to like a human being.

It takes confidence to be a great conversationalist, to really listen to someone speaking without judgment or the influence of the ego. These kinds of high quality conversations are not easy to come by but I am trying every day to be as present as I can with whomever I am speaking to. In conversations where both people are present, we're not just talking about ourselves, but we're seeing one another for who we truly are. That is a deeply spiritual experience. You can't truly listen to someone if you're constantly deciding if you agree and disagree with everything that they say. You're not listening at all. You're just judging. We must all learn to listen without judgment. That is true conversation.

:|| 34 ||:

Relentless Optimism

"Where there is love there is life."

– Mahatma Gandhi

I know my journey is only at the very beginning. There is so much yet to see, so much yet to experience, so many people who will go on to change my life. Time is already starting to fly and it will continue to fly. That's a sign, I think, that life is captivating and entertaining you! I've been really fortunate to be inspired and loved by so many wonderful people. I'm fortunate that these people have all contributed, one way or another, to my life as a young musician and that I've got a shot at what I believe is the greatest job anyone could ever have – playing jazz violin for people around the world.

I said in the beginning of this book that I saw my life in two parts. Part one started when I was born and lasted until I moved away from home. Part two started after I moved away from home and I think it has just ended. It feels as though part three has started now. As I write this, I'm reflecting on the week that I spent in New Orleans recording my fourth album, and those recording sessions have given me a new belief in myself and in music that I never had before. I feel free. I feel alive. I feel the power of love and the power of music in a new way.

It was an honor to record my own songs, songs I wrote the music and lyrics and arrangements for myself, and to play with such incredible musicians and in such a wonderful city and recording studio. Martin Taylor and I played a duet together, one that he sent me from his home studio in Scotland. Evan Christopher, Marshall Hawkins' first jazz student, also played on one of the tracks. Although everyone in the band and in the studio was a joy to work with, I was especially moved by getting to work with the bassist Roland Guerin and drummer Jamison Ross, two of New Orleans' greatest musicians.

Roland's life-loving spirit as a bassist and friend uplifted me and continually inspires me to be and play like myself. Jamison Ross, who more than deserves his recent Grammy nomination for his first solo album, also gave me great musical and creative encouragement. His example of compassion and positivity is something to strive for.

One of the greatest lessons I learned while visiting New Orleans was about insecurity. I'm mentioning this now, towards the end of the book, because it's one of the most profound lessons I've stumbled on in my life so far, and it's something I wanted you to remember this book by. So here I go. While I was in town, Roland Guerin was playing a Christmas show at Snug Harbor, one of New Orleans' most famous jazz venues, with a wonderful singer Philip Manuel. I'd never met Philip before or been to Snug Harbor, but at the intermission, Roland introduced me to Philip. Philip asked me if I brought my violin and of course I did, so he invited me up to play with the band for the second set.

I thought I'd just be playing along with Philip and what they had already rehearsed, but Philip went a step further and asked me if I'd like to do my own little feature with the band without him on stage at all. I said I'd be honored to and thanked him for being so gracious, but I had to ask him this. I said, "Philip, you've never heard me play before. How do you know I won't mess up your whole show? How can you feel comfortable just turning it over to me without even thinking about it?" He said, "Listen, baby, I've got no insecurities. Not even one."

In that moment, something really hit me. He couldn't be humiliated because of me no matter what I did because he wasn't connected to the outcome of what I was doing. There was no way for me to embarrass him because he didn't have anything to be insecure about. Now I fully understood something fundamental about life. If you let go of your insecurities, nobody can make you look or feel bad. It just won't stick to you. Everyone is free to do what he or she wants to do and nobody is afraid to let anyone else down.

But here's one more thing to it – it's not just that Philip had no insecurities. This feeling spread to me as well! Suddenly I had no insecurities either! If he trusted me, why shouldn't *I* trust me? I naturally walked on stage with all of the confidence in the world and played well because I truly thought that there was no way this could go wrong. I wasn't insecure, Philip wasn't insecure, and my violin wasn't insecure either. Everything just flowed freely. The audience wasn't insecure, the band wasn't insecure, even the rats in the alley outside weren't insecure, all because this one guy had told me, "Hey. Go do your thing. Have some fun on my stage. Don't worry about me."

If there's just one person who I must thank for everything, including this book, it's Marshall. Without his guidance and love none of this would have happened to me. I admire him so much for his dedication to bringing jazz to young people everywhere, his way of teaching that bestows equal parts responsibility and freedom onto his students, his commitment to improving his playing and performing with no plan to ever stop, but most importantly, for his ability to see within young people talent and potential that we can't always see ourselves. He looked at us as if he were saying, "You have no idea how amazing you are. But I'm going to show you." And that made him amazing to us. His ability as a mentor has changed a lot of lives including mine. I feel nothing but pure love.

Real love for someone, whether it's a family member or a friend or a lover or even your dog means that you want to cherish and be around that person whenever he or she is near. You want to give that person a hug, hold his or her hand, you want to treat that person with respect and look him or her in the eye. You want to be fully present and to give love freely.

Keep the people who you feel real love for around you as much as possible and tell them how much you love them. Real love doesn't make you feel trapped, guilty, or at fault for anything – love doesn't make you feel afraid or scared or doomed or inadequate or burdened. Real love makes you feel free. Real love makes you feel like yourself. That's the kind of love we should all search for and give to one another, just like Philip and Marshall gave to me.

The world is like a river. What will you contribute to the river? Clean water or something else? We are all drinking from and giving back to the same life river. So as you look around at the supermarket, when you're at the park or a concert, in your classroom or in your house, think about what you are giving to the river. And if you are drinking poisoned water, the best way to cure yourself is to put pure water back into the river as much as you can.

And to everyone in the world, strangers and friends alike, why not give love freely? When we all work together, we can transform anything! Compassion for the self, for others and for the Earth can solve anything. Why not be a part of someone achieving something amazing? Why not give your love away for free? Don't worry about if someone deserves it or if he or she is worthy of it. If you can give that person something precious, give it away. If you can give someone encouragement, a little moment or a little piece of your heart then do it.

Why not see just how amazing you can make someone else's life? Get on the love train! And don't just get on it when there are celebrities or people you look up to around you. You can be on the love train when you're talking to strangers too, people who have lives on the other side of the world or who work in professions you didn't know existed.

Why not see just how amazing your own life can be? Sometimes these things can surprise you. Well, I'm open to being surprised. *Life, I hope you're listening.* Surprise me. Show me how amazing it can all be. I'm not thinking small. I want you to amaze me and astound me. I am open. Life is constant evolution. I feel in favor with the universe. I am part of the universal flow. What we say it will be is what it is.

I can already see that what life offers us is often beyond anything we can comprehend on our own, even in our wildest dreams. But that's how life works. It's often more amazing than anything we could possibly conceive of. All we need to do is keep our hearts and minds open. Well I'm ready. How can it get better than this?

About the Author

Nora Germain is a jazz violinist, recording artist, author, bandleader, and songwriter currently residing in Los Angeles, California. At age 24 she has already released four of her own albums and has performed with an impressive list of renowned musical artists including Tommy Emmanuel CGP, Martin Taylor MBE, Jon Batiste and Stay Human, Evan Christopher, Jacob Collier, Alison Burns, John Altman, Casey Abrams, Marshall Hawkins, and Sam Smith. She has been featured on a wide array of soundtracks for TV and film as well as on albums for artists from around the globe. She has also played for numerous charities and organizations including Children's Hospital in Los Angeles, where she played on a weekly basis from 2014-2016.

www.noragermain.com